# Praise for *Never Cold Call Ag...*

"Cold calling has the lowest percentage of sales call s... ... ... you in-vest the same amount of time in reading this book as you do in cold calling, your success percentage and your income will skyrocket."

—Jeffrey Gitomer, Author of
*The Little Red Book of Selling*

"I don't know about you, but I sure never buy from a cold call. Heck, I'll have fun with the cold caller in hopes of scaring him into another, less annoying, job. Frank's extremely detailed book will introduce you to a new way of doing business that should break your company of the cold-calling addiction and simultaneously increase your sales."

—Mark Joyner, Author of *The Irresistible Offer*

"You can never get enough of a good thing! Read this book and use its contents!"

—Anthony Parinello, Best-Selling Author of
*Selling to VITO* and *Stop Cold Calling Forever*

"Stop wondering what makes that other guy successful and start imple-menting some of Frank's proven strategies. This book will earn you thousands more this year and open your eyes to the biggest deals in the world."

—Daniel Waldschmidt, CEO, ACCESS Litigation
Support Services, www.accesslitigation.com

"If you're demanding that your salespeople make cold calls, you need this book. Frank Rumbauskas has created an outstanding plan that eliminates cold calls and increases your team's effectiveness while in-creasing your corporate sales figures."

—Leslie Hughes, President, Corporate Moves, Inc.,
www.CMISearch.com

"I've been using these concepts for my team of insurance agents. We now have a national presence and have been able to accomplish this while increasing profitability for the company, and more importantly for the agents in the street."

—Jeff McElroy, President, JD McElroy Financial
Advisors LLC, www.jeffmcelroy.com

"After implementing just a few of your techniques, I went from signing 5 to 8 clients per month to signing 16 to 20. When I finally caught my breath, I tried some of your other tips and last month alone added over 100 new clients!"

—Kathy Harper, United BankCard,
www.freecreditcardterminalsite.com

"The best sales professionals in the world are going nowhere without the proper number of qualified prospects to speak with. Using Frank's systems, I now have my ideal prospects seeking me out. One simple strategy grew my e-mail newsletter last month alone by 948 people . . . who all sought me out as the expert. Thanks, Frank!"

—Tom Beal, Sales Coach,
www.THESalesChampion.com

"My interpretation of *Never Cold Call Again* is that most salespeople need a marketing program. I think your advice is extremely practical and important for 95 percent of the salespeople out there (myself included as a small business owner) who cannot rely on their marketing department to supply the leads they need to fill their sales funnel."

—Nigel Edelshain, President, Ivy Tech Partners,
and Chairman, Wharton Business School Club
of New York, www.itsalesideas.com

"I ordered Frank's course 'in the blind.' I am a very satisfied customer. I have increased my business and destressed my life using some of Frank's cogent tips and techniques. He's a man who delivers on his promises."

—David W. Starr, Vice President, SatViz Inc.,
www.SatViz.com

# NEVER COLD CALL AGAIN!

*Achieve Sales Greatness without Cold Calling*

FRANK J. RUMBAUSKAS JR.

**WILEY**

John Wiley & Sons, Inc.

Published by John Wiley & Sons, Inc., Hoboken, New Jersey.
Published simultaneously in Canada.

For general information on our other products and services or for technical support, please contact our Customer Care Department within the United States at (800) 762-2974, outside the United States at (317) 572-3993 or fax (317) 572-4002.

Wiley also publishes its books in a variety of electronic formats. Some content that appears in print may not be available in electronic books. For more information about Wiley products, visit our web site at www.wiley.com.

*Library of Congress Cataloging-in-Publication Data:*
Rumbauskas, Frank J., 1973-
    Never cold call again! Achieve sales greatness without cold calling / Frank J. Rumbauskas Jr.
        p.   cm.
    Includes index.
    ISBN-13: 978-0-471-78679-5 (pbk.)
    ISBN-10: 0-471-78679-9 (pbk.)
    1. Selling.   2. Selling—Technological innovations.   I. Title.
    HF5438.25.R85 2006
    658.85—dc22

                                                                    2005027607

Printed in the United States of America.

10   9   8   7   6   5   4   3   2   1

*To my father,*

from whom I learned the entrepreneurial spirit at a very young age,

and

*to my mother,*

who always knew I'd succeed no matter what stood in my way.

# CONTENTS

# PREFACE

When new to sales, I followed the advice provided to me by both company training and various books and tapes on the subject. That advice was to prospect via cold calling. I was taught to use both telephone and in-person cold calling, or "pounding the pavement," and that it was the honorable thing that hardworking salespeople did to succeed.

Even though it worked for a while, I always had to struggle to make my numbers that way. All too often, I didn't make my numbers at all, and I eventually became frustrated altogether with cold calling. My first few years in sales were an endless pattern of warning, final warning, fired, new job, warning, final warning, fired, and on and on. I continued to follow the standard advice of "cold call more" and "increase your activity," and I kept hitting a brick wall. The more people I asked for help, the more I heard those overused clichés, and the more failure I encountered. I soon realized that my managers and trainers couldn't help me. After all, they had heard those same exact words all through their careers. The problem was that it worked in their day, but it doesn't work anymore. However, too many people cling to old ideas that they're comfortable with—the sales profession is notorious for this—and I never received any advice that could really help me.

Finally, I had the good fortune to be hired by my first good manager, who really believed that prospecting and cold calling should be left to low-paid telemarketers while the talented sales force spent their time closing the qualified leads that are generated as a result. Unfortunately, that particular company didn't provide the necessary funds and structure to allow this manager to hire those telemarketers. What did happen, however, was that we as salespeople really embraced this concept and set out on our own to figure out ways to automatically generate leads without the difficult, boring, and very time-consuming task of cold calling.

Over a period of several years I experimented with different methods, spent time with successful salespeople, and eventually built a self-marketing system consisting of several simple yet effective marketing techniques that cost little or nothing to implement. The best part was that my system had a cumulative effect. In other words, I kept getting more and more leads as time went on, and before long I was able to stop cold calling entirely. It even got to the point where I could select the prospects I wanted to work with and qualify-out those who weren't worth my time. In several instances I simply referred them to other sales reps and split the commission. Talk about easy money. To this day I still get phone calls from prospects who are looking to buy something, despite the fact that it's been at least three years since my last active self-marketing campaign. This is the powerful cumulative effect I'm talking about.

As my learning curve continued, I noticed a strange circumstance in that the sales process with these marketing-generated leads was quite different from those I'd previously uncovered through cold calling. The dynamic that was different at the very beginning continued all the way through the sales process. I found that many of the sales techniques in those books that told me to cold call didn't work on these prospects who had come to me through my self-marketing program. Many of the traditional sales techniques are intended for prospects who have less than a 50 percent chance of buying and therefore really need to be sold. However, highly qualified prospects who contact you in response to a well-executed self-marketing campaign are put off by typical sales tactics.

It is for that reason that this book presents an entire system of selling, rather than merely providing a list of prospecting and marketing techniques. While that is certainly the focus of much of this book, you need to understand the different dynamic at work with these prospects who respond to your marketing efforts and call you first. The selling process is very different from what you're used to experiencing with prospects uncovered via cold calling. While prospects who come into contact with a salesperson through cold calling have a tendency to be skeptical and sometimes even disrespectful of that salesperson, prospects have a much higher level of trust and respect for salespeople whom they called first. You'll learn how to use this to your advantage and induce prospects to buy from you without the need for high-pressure tactics or closes on your part. You'll learn how to present yourself as an authority figure who can fulfill their needs instead of a hungry salesperson who is in need.

As the first chapter explains, times have changed, and old Industrial Age sales techniques have become ineffective and even counterproductive in our new Information Age, twenty-first century economy. The sad truth is that the vast majority of the sales profession is stuck in the Industrial Age. By learning this information now, you'll easily move ahead and rise to the top in the field of selling, and you'll experience far less stress than when you did things the old way.

# Part One

---

# A NEW WAY OF SELLING

# 1

## TIMES HAVE CHANGED: WELCOME TO THE INFORMATION AGE

**A BACKGROUND ON SELLING IN THE NEW ECONOMY**

The world of selling hasn't changed much in recent years, while the world of business in general has changed dramatically. I continue to see the same old advice, instructions, and clichés that were taught decades ago being used today. This is the primary reason why more salespeople than ever are struggling to survive, while the few who have learned to embrace new ideas are moving ahead by leaps and bounds.

Many historians use the fall of the Berlin Wall in 1989 to mark the end of the Industrial Age and the beginning of the Information Age. In so many areas of business the shift has been dramatic, most notably in our global economy. Computers and technology have taken quantum leaps forward, and the Internet has forever changed the way we communicate and do business.

However, one area of business has been remarkably stagnant and continues to fiercely resist the change into the Information Age. That area is sales.

One recent example of what I'm talking about stands out in my mind. A friend of mine who worked alongside me in sales recently took a job with a large, well-known corporation. He was always a top producer—innovative, efficient, and consistently over 150 percent of quota. He understood the proper use of marketing and consequently attained his high results without cold calling.

He was stunned when he was told that he would be required to make an absolute minimum of 400 in-person cold calls each week, and to provide 400 new business cards each week as proof that he had made his calls. He was also required to carry a demonstration kit and to be pushy and try to perform demonstrations of the company's product as often as possible on that first—and usually unwelcome—visit.

Because this individual knows how to sell in ways that are far more efficient than this, he approached his manager to discuss various strategies that he'd effectively used in the past to achieve his high results. The manager's answer? "We've done it this way for 40 years, and we're not about to change."

In my opinion, that answer explains why so many salespeople are struggling to make a living. When you consider the massive changes we've experienced in this shift to the Information Age, common sense says that anything that was effective 40 years ago cannot possibly work today.

I honestly believe that this clinging to old, obsolete ideas is the main reason we're seeing record business bankruptcies today.

One of the keys to success in sales in today's economy is to keep an open mind to new ideas. It's obvious that the people I'm talking about here are not open-minded whatsoever, and in fact are very close-minded. They were taught all the right answers, but unfortunately, their once-right answers are now very wrong.

It reminds me of a true story I once heard about Albert Einstein when he was teaching as a professor. A student assistant was about to prepare a test for the next class. He asked, "Professor Einstein, which test are we giving them?" To which Einstein replied, "The same test as last week." The assistant, bewildered, asked, "But why give them the same test again?" To which Einstein replied, "Because the answers are different this week."

In our fast-moving, evolving new world, we may continue to face all the same challenges, but the answers are constantly changing. If you do not continue your learning curve, always remaining open-minded to new ideas, you will be left behind. Those who continually adapt themselves to new ideas are quickly getting ahead, while those who insist on clinging to their old, right answers have become obsolete.

You'll need to keep an open mind as you learn the material in this book. Before you can accept, learn, and use the ideas and techniques put forth herein, your mind must be ready and willing to accept them. Remember that as you read and think about how you'll apply the material in your day-to-day selling.

# 2

## WHY SELLING IS OUT AND SELF-MARKETING IS IN

### SELLING IN TODAY'S WORLD

Once upon a time, advertising was a novel and entertaining thing. Families would excitedly gather around the television just for the commercials, anxiously waiting to see which of their favorite stars would appear in the new ones. Instead of an annoying distraction, commercials were seen as a fun diversion, something to smile and laugh at and, as a result, they were highly effective at selling products.

What's today's view of commercials? Who really pays attention anymore? Most of us start flipping channels, trying to find another without commercials. Advertisers continue to see a rapid decline in the effectiveness of their ads and are scrambling to find alternative ways to attract new customers. Many industry experts are even predicting that most of the big-name, multibillion dollar advertising agencies will be out of business by the end of the decade.

Seth Godin made the distinction in his book *Permission Marketing* perhaps better than anyone else has. He calls the old, intrusive methods of advertising "interruption marketing" and talks about the importance of inducing customers to come to you and volunteer to hear what you have to say, or "permission marketing." With that in mind, let's consider cold calling.

Cold calling is the salesperson's equivalent of interruption marketing. Think about it: When you make a cold call, either in person or on the phone, you're interrupting someone. In today's world, we've become practically immune to the endless buzz of advertising. How many do you really pay attention to? Think of all the TV commercials, radio ads, magazine and newspaper ads, billboards, signs everywhere on storefronts, roadsides, and on buses and taxis, and all those pushy salespeople looking to sell you something. We've even built sales resistance to the nice people offering free samples in the supermarket. It's become too much, and nearly all of us have a built-in defense mechanism to advertising and salespeople.

As we move further into the twenty-first century, cold calling is not only losing its effectiveness but is getting to the point where it's actually becoming counterproductive. It annoys people. It wastes people's time. It has a great chance of turning off someone who might have been a good prospect and who would have probably bought from you if you had contacted that person in a more legitimate manner.

## WHY COLD CALLING DOESN'T WORK ANYMORE

Let's explore some of the key reasons why traditional cold calling has become obsolete and ineffective in today's economy:

### *Cold Calling Destroys Your Status as a Business Equal*

In order to be successful in today's world of ever-increasing sales resistance, you need to project a very strong image of confidence and success and the perception that you do not need the prospect's business. Most of us have heard about the importance of being willing to walk, but how can you possibly emanate these qualities when you put yourself into a cold call situation? You can't! When you make a cold call, it's very obvious to the prospect that you need their business. All the power shifts to the prospect right from the very start, and it's extremely difficult to get that power back later on. Keeping your power throughout the sales process is extremely important and is discussed in greater detail later on.

Another thing we've all undoubtedly noticed is how top producers are quick to decorate their office walls, business cards, and stationery with their awards. We've all met salespeople with such things as President's Club printed in gold foil on their cards. Why? Because it shows that they do not need business, and this makes prospects want to do business with them! That's why so many business owners who call in requesting information will ask to speak with a manager or with the owner of the company.

Cold calling creates the perception that you have nothing else going on, and nothing more important to do than go out and try to scrape up some business.

### *Cold Calling Limits Production and Earnings Potential*

One of the most important concepts you must understand in order to be successful in our new Information Age economy is the concept of leverage.

The problem with cold calling is that it is a one-to-one occurrence. In other words, you can make only one phone call at a time, or knock on one door at a time. What's more, it happens only when you're actively doing it. Anytime you're not cold calling, no progress is being made. If you have a great month and earn a big commission check as a result of cold calling, you still have to start all over again from zero next month and go back to making those calls, one at a time.

By using leverage, on the other hand, you can increase your prospecting power exponentially. The key to successfully using leverage lies in systems. By building individual systems to generate leads for you, then integrating those individual systems into one main system of systems, you can attain massive results.

For a better understanding of what a system of systems really is, look at an automobile. A car is one large system of about a dozen individual systems working together in harmony. The engine is one system. The transmission is another. The brakes are another. Steering is a system. Put together, they make a car that gets you from point A to point B safely and reliably. A jet aircraft is a more complicated example. It consists of literally hundreds of individual systems, but like a car, when those systems are put together into one main system, they work in harmony to produce the desired result of safe, fast, reliable air transportation.

The perfect example of the opposite of using leveraged systems in sales is the classic sales training explanation of how to plan your activity. It goes something like this: "Take your quota and divide it by the average dollar amount per sale to determine how many sales you need each month. Now multiply that number by the number of proposals you need to present in order to get a sale. Multiply that number by the number of initial appointments it takes you to get to the proposal stage. Finally, multiply that number by the number of cold calls it takes you to get an appointment. Now you know how many cold calls you must make every month. Divide the total by 20 working days, and you now know your minimum daily activity in cold calling."

This method of activity planning contains a number of fatal flaws. The most obvious one is that it limits your production by time. Salespeople who are brutally honest about how many cold calls are necessary to get a qualified lead—not a time waster—and how many of those appointments actually result in sales, will find that there simply aren't enough hours in the day to do that many cold calls and still have time for first appointments, follow-up appointments, proposal generation, and so on. This method of activity planning fails to incorporate any means of leverage. It leaves the salesperson with no system and a very inefficient plan to get new business.

Leverage, on the other hand, not only multiplies your prospecting power dramatically, but also frees up a lot of your valuable time. Once your prospecting system is built, you no longer have to spend hours and hours every day cold calling. You can devote your time to more productive and worthwhile activities.

### Cold Calling Makes Timing Work Against You

It does you no good to spend time with a prospect who has no current need for your product, may have a need in the distant future but not right now, is already a customer of your company, or who has just bought from your competition.

The problem with cold calling is that it leaves timing entirely to chance. When you call someone or walk into their door at random, you have absolutely no idea whether they have a current need for your product or service. Cold calling forces you to waste time on people who will not buy from you, no matter what.

Doctors don't call you at random trying to set appointments. Neither do auto mechanics; can you imagine one saying, "Hello, when could you bring your car in for us to look at and determine if we may be of service to you at all?" It sounds silly, but this is what most prospects think when you propose that same question.

Nothing irritates a busy executive more than wasted time. If you call someone or barge into their office unannounced, the chances are slim that you can possibly be of any benefit to them, and as a result, you have wasted their time and yours. This may anger an important prospect who otherwise may have been willing to talk to you at some point in the future. When I was out cold calling trying to sell phone systems, it never occurred to me that businesses buy new phone systems, on average, every seven years. And yet these poor decision makers get a dozen calls a week from salespeople trying to "set a time to assess your needs and determine if we may be of service to you." It doesn't work. One trainer I had when I was new in sales pointed out the fact that 20 years ago, prospects would invite you in for a cup of coffee and appreciate the information. Today, that isn't the case. In fact, the shouts of "No soliciting!" were common, and I distinctly remember one incident when the police were called and I barely avoided arrest for violating a no soliciting sign.

### Cold Calling Fails to Find the Prequalified Prospects We All Need

This fact can be confirmed by analyzing the close ratio data for leads generated through cold calling compared with leads generated through all other sources. I remember the point in my sales career when it finally hit me that cold calling took up 80 percent of my free selling time, and yet accounted for only about 10 percent of my sales. All the rest came from marketing efforts, networking, and referrals. It amazed me how the cold call generated leads were more than happy to meet with me and waste my time, yet few ever bought. They were the ones who were notorious for saying, "This looks great, we think we'll do it," then never returning another phone call.

The fact is that most busy, successful businesspeople, the ones we really want as customers, don't take cold calls and don't meet with salespeople unless they requested the meeting themselves. This leaves the time wasters we know all too well. Furthermore, if you happen to uncover a prospect via cold calling who is actually in a buying cycle for your product, chances are they've already met with some of your competitors, already have proposals on the table, and you're late to the game.

Take a look at the dynamics of what happens when a salesperson makes a cold call, and think about what must go through a prospect's mind that causes them to reject the salesperson. When we make that call, we usually hope and expect that the prospect will at least be somewhat receptive to hearing what we have to say. However, salespeople increasingly face resistance to cold calling, as well as increasing flakiness on the part of prospects who do accept cold calls, say they'll meet with you, and then not show up for appointments, and so on.

Instead of thinking, "Okay, this may be of value," here is what most prospects actually think when they receive a cold call: "Great. You don't know me and I don't know you. You have no idea what my company does or what my own goals are. You don't even know if we need whatever it is you're selling, and in spite of all this, you've decided to waste my time anyway."

What is increasingly becoming the norm is to be rejected by the good, solid prospects everybody wants, and to get appointments with time wasters who will never buy anything. Flakiness is a growing problem thanks to the fact that prospects are constantly bombarded with both advertising and sales calls. When you consider the fact that few prospects actually have the courage to say no, it's more important than ever to make sure you're dealing only with highly qualified prospects.

### Cold Calling Puts You in a Negative Light and Annoys People

As I mentioned earlier, nothing angers a busy decision maker more than a waste of valuable time. Think about what it's like to be buried under a pile of paperwork, facing endless meetings and hoping you get out of the office in time for dinner, when your phone rings and you hear a salesperson on the other end trying to get an appointment and hitting you with a pushy tactic like, "Is Wednesday or next Monday better for you?" Obviously, it's annoying and disrespectful, and all it really does is get you on the bad side of someone who otherwise might have bought from you.

### Cold Calling Might Get You in Trouble

I already mentioned the time I narrowly avoided jail for making a cold call. It's also worthy of mention that my home state requires you to get a Telephone Solicitor's License before making a cold call to anyone, residential or business, and that many other states have similar regulations. Tolerance for cold calling is diminishing, and "do not call" is just the beginning.

### *Salespeople Hate Cold Calling!*

Forget all the other reasons. Even if it worked, who wants to do something they hate? One of the keys to being successful in your job is to make it fun! Even the most goofy, rah-rah trainers and coaches will readily admit that nobody likes to cold call. So don't do something that will ruin your attitude.

### BUYING VERSUS SELLING

In addition to understanding and accepting the fact that cold calling is no longer the answer, you must understand the difference between *buying* and *selling* as they relate here. Here is how I define them in today's world:

- *Buying*: The act of willingly purchasing something that one wants or needs. The buyer leaves the transaction feeling satisfied and fulfilled.
- *Selling*: Attempting to convince another that they want or need your product regardless of whether they do or not. The buyer frequently experiences buyer's remorse after such a transaction.

Can you see how cold calling causes selling to take place, while using leveraged systems to attract qualified prospects causes buying to take place?

Keep the term "causes to take place" in mind all along. The goal of this system of selling is to cause buying to take place instead of attempting to force selling to take place. By using leveraged systems of self-marketing, you will induce qualified prospects who need your product to come to you and buy.

Let's look at an example where cold calling actually resulted in a sale, for example "selling":

The customer receives a cold call from a salesperson, and after numerous callbacks an initial appointment is set. The prospect has a high level of sales resistance. After all, the salesperson is someone who called hoping to make a sale, and sales pressure is expected. The usual fact finding takes place, and a time is set to return with a proposal.

The day of the second appointment arrives, and the prospect has an even higher level of sales resistance; this is a proposal appointment, and the salesperson will try to close the sale. The presentation takes place, the customer tells the salesperson what their decision process is and promises to call when they've made a decision. The salesperson jumps the gun and calls a few days later to ask "if a decision has been made." Obviously it hasn't; otherwise the prospect would have called.

The customer finally decides to buy, the contract is signed, and a delivery date is set. The customer can't help but wonder if they got the best deal and how things will go with their new purchase.

Can you feel the tension throughout that whole process? By contrast, let's look at a situation where "buying" took place:

The prospect contacts the salesperson as a result of the salesperson's self-marketing efforts. The customer recognizes the product or service being offered by this sales rep as something they may need, and the initial call is made. The customer's frame of mind is now set and will carry through the entire sales process. By calling you, the customer is automatically slotted into the position of needing something that you can provide. On the other hand, if you make a cold call to the customer, you are the one in need and they become the provider. This is why attracting customers through self-marketing is far more effective than cold calling.

After the salesperson asks some questions in an attempt to qualify the prospect out, the salesperson agrees to visit with the customer at a time convenient to the salesperson.

The initial appointment takes place, and the customer looks forward to it because they already know they have a need, unlike an appointment set through cold calling where the prospect may be unsure as to what the call is even about. The salesperson shows up looking very professional, emanating an aura of success. The standard questioning process takes place and the customer's needs are voiced. The salesperson may ask more qualifying questions, to further reinforce the psychology of placing the customer in a position of needing to gain the salesperson's acceptance.

The salesperson returns for a second meeting with a proposal and contracts. This proposal is strictly relevant to the customer's needs and does not contain a company story or the CEO's bio unless the customer specifically requests it. Price objections usually do not take place because the initial qualifying and questioning process was designed to eliminate them from the beginning. Contracts are signed and delivery is scheduled. Note that no "closes" were used. Because the salesperson conducted the sale from a position of authority and in a manner relevant to the customer's needs, the customer naturally bought.

The customer is satisfied and excited about their new purchase, and gladly offers referrals upon being asked.

Notice how much easier the second example is for the salesperson. None of the stereotypical sales tactics such as the "alternative close" were used. It was a very natural, positive experience for the customer, and they really feel that the salesperson has helped them.

Keep this distinction between "buying" and "selling" in mind as you read this book and apply it.

Consider the purchases you've made. Take a minute or two to think about everything you've bought recently. Now think about the advertising you're hit with every day, and the calls you've received from salespeople. Have any of your significant purchases resulted from those interruption marketing approaches? Probably not. Right now I'm thinking of all the products and services I've purchased within my company, and none of them were the result of an unsolicited sales call. Ironically, I've received cold calls from people selling some of the exact same things I've bought, but unfortunately timing worked against them. Calling people at random is horribly inefficient and difficult compared to using leveraged self-marketing systems to bring qualified prospects to you.

## SELLING IS SELLING

Of all the calls and e-mails I get from salespeople who are searching for a better way, the most common of all is, "I sell _____. Will your methods work for me?"

What salespeople must realize is that all selling is really the same regardless of what your product is. One of the single most frustrating things I experienced in my sales career was the answer I got every time I tried to change industries. It was always, "You apparently have a proven track record of success, but without experience in our industry, we can't hire you."

This drove me crazy because I knew that selling is selling, but it was all but impossible to convince managers of this. People are people and human nature is always the same, regardless of what you happen to be selling or what industry you're in. I know of people who have been highly successful in a variety of totally unrelated fields, and I also know people who have been miserable failures in several fields. It doesn't matter. One of the mistakes I made early on in selling was to assume that something that had been highly effective for someone in another industry wouldn't work for me. Not so. The only thing that really changes from industry to industry is product knowledge, which is a lot easier to learn than selling, and which isn't as important as people seem to think it is if they have their selling skills in order.

Early on I'd meet a successful salesperson, find out what they were doing that was working, and say, "That may work for you, but it wouldn't work for my product." That was a terrible mistake on my part and I hope that other salespeople won't make that mistake themselves. As you read and learn this material, understand that it will work for you, and take the time to attend networking events where you can associate with and learn from salespeople in different industries. You may be surprised to see how much you can learn from them. You'll pick up some new ideas that nobody in your company has thought of and that can propel you on to greater success.

## SELLING IS STUPID

While that title may be offensive to some, and for good reason, that's not the case when you consider my definition of "selling." There are too many easier ways to get business than to fight an uphill battle, trying to sell and close people.

The reason there is so much emphasis in modern sales training to do proper follow-ups with customers after a sale in order to alleviate buyer's remorse is because the poor customers are being coerced into selling situations, rather than induced to buy. Think about every action you take in your day-to-day sales and whether it constitutes selling or buying.

This shift in the world of selling really should come as no surprise. Change and the evolution of ideas are an integral part of capitalism. Yet this very feature of capitalism is destroying those who resist it. It was best explained by Dr. Joseph A. Schumpeter, the former Austrian minister of finance and Harvard Business School professor. He described capitalism as "creative destruction." In other words, capitalism is a perpetual cycle of destroying old, less-efficient businesses and ideas and replacing them with new, more-efficient ones. This feature of capitalism is inevitable and unavoidable, and is the reason why only those who are willing to adapt to changing times can possibly survive.

The bottom line is that selling is out, and using leveraged systems of self-marketing is in. That's what works today, and that's what will generate the huge sales results we all want.

# 3

## OLD ANSWERS ARE WRONG ANSWERS

Those "old, right answers" that are very wrong today are still touted as the right answers even though results prove otherwise. Here are the most common ones:

- "It's a numbers game." The most common "old, right answer" is the myth that sales is a numbers game. Sales is not a numbers game. If something isn't working, doing it over and over again definitely isn't going to work. If one thing doesn't work, the result is zero. If you try it 50 times, 50 times 0 equals 0. It's been said that the definition of insanity is doing the same thing over and over and expecting different results.

  One of the most frustrating things I experienced early on in sales was my disappointment with getting poor results from cold calling, yet every time I approached a manager for advice, the answer I got was, "Increase your activity." In other words, they were telling me to do even more of what wasn't working! That never made any sense to me, and I'm amazed that this idea is still encouraged today.

  That seems to be the standard end-all and be-all answer from the majority of sales managers and trainers. "Increase your activity." "Cold call more." "Your activity isn't there." Unfortunately, these people fail to realize that doing more of something that isn't working gets only more poor results. Why this myth continues to live on is a mystery to me. All I can think of is the simple fact that nobody is ever taught anything different.

- "Be persistent." A close relative to the "numbers game" myth is persistence. The problem with persistence is that, while it is a good virtue in and of itself, dwelling on it usually forces salespeople to waste time with worthless prospects instead of writing them off and moving on to more profitable ones.

The most annoying thing a salesperson can do to a prospect is to keep calling to find out if a decision has been made. Think back to my definitions of selling and buying. In the selling situation, the salesperson irritates the prospect by calling too soon and asking, "Have you made a decision yet?" This is not only annoying and somewhat disrespectful to the prospect, but it is a waste of time and only serves to negatively affect your attitude. If they've made a decision to buy, they'll call you. I've never known a prospect who wanted to buy who didn't call. I remember times when I was on vacation and had three or four voice mails when I returned from a prospect who had decided to buy and was now anxious to get moving. On the other hand, we all pretty much know the sad reality that most prospects who have made a decision not to buy do not have the courage to say no. Instead, they choose to avoid you and hope you'll get the hint. Unfortunately, most salespeople don't get the hint, and continue calling and leaving messages. If you've left several messages for a prospect who hasn't called back, it's safe to say they're not going to buy. While you're spending time chasing a dead lead, your competitors are out finding the good prospects who will buy.

Another part of the problem with being too persistent and wasting time on bad prospects is the effect that these deals have on overbearing managers if you happen to leave them on your forecast, which brings us to the next topic.

- "Funnels and forecasts." Sales forecasts and funnels are a great idea in theory. Any well-managed business must have accurate forecasting in order to effect proper planning. In addition, salespeople and managers must keep track of their sales funnels in order to properly manage themselves and their time.

The problems begin when salespeople and managers misuse and abuse these tools, and that's almost always the case.

Consider forecasts. How many salespeople actually forecast accurately? In my experience, the answer is few, if any at all. No salesperson wants to submit a forecast that falls short, so they embellish existing deals or leave in dead deals just to have enough. The result is that the forecasts are never accurate, and therefore become useless to everyone involved and adversely affect business planning.

Then there's the opposite misuse of forecasts, the one I was always guilty of. As a salesperson, there was nothing in the world I hated more than a manager who would breathe down my neck day after day, going down the list and asking me when each one of the deals was going to sign, and putting constant pressure on me to close them. This is what I was referring to when I said that persistence can be counterproductive as it relates to forecasts. What I've found is that many managers believe in persistence to an extreme, for example calling prospects every day until they either say yes or no. I distinctly remember managers touting this belief and even requiring us to call every single prospect on the forecast daily and pester them to buy. You can guess what the outcome was—a lot of infuriated prospects who swore never to do business with us, and of course, the managers always blamed the salespeople for this. I even remember one manager who had a "10 percent rule": nobody was allowed to deviate more than 10 percent from their forecasted number every week, and anyone who did was in big trouble. We even got into trouble for *exceeding* our forecasts by more than 10 percent!

Considering funnels, there are two reasons that lead me to believe they are also counterproductive and of little use to salespeople, at least the way they're traditionally used. The first problem is that the word "funnel" is usually equated with poor performance and probation. Just hearing the word sends chills down the spines of most salespeople and negatively affects their attitudes.

The real problem with funnels, though, is that "funnel management" is nothing more than another way of saying, "Increase your activity," and we've already learned why the myth of "increase your activity" is a wrong answer. All funnel management really does is keep track of how much business you have in the various stages of the sales cycle. For example, you might have 20 prospects in the lead stage, 10 in the proposal stage, 5 in the contracts stage, and so on. Does this sound familiar? It's basically a graphical presentation of the old-school sales activity plan of "Multiply this by that and the other thing."

Sales managers usually refer to funnel management by saying such things as, "You need to have at least 500 percent of your quota in the proposal stage every month." All this says is, "Increase your activity." My argument against this is that there are a lot of reasons for poor sales attainment other than a lack of activity, such as dealing with unqualified prospects, carrying out an improper sales process, poor presentation (of both yourself personally and your products), and so on. Focusing on funnel management, a.k.a. activity, causes one to overlook these more important selling skills.

• "Dress like your prospects." Of all the myths out there, I think this is one of the most dangerous of all and is causing entirely too many salespeople to give away their power and lose deals without any apparent explanation.

One of the key concepts I teach salespeople is to avoid giving away their power. They must keep their power at all times. As soon as you give your power away to a prospect, you lose control of the sales situation, and it's almost impossible to reverse it and regain control.

Dressing like your prospects is the absolute last thing you should do. You should dress like the people they turn to for advice. By doing this, you help to put yourself into the coveted position of being an authority figure to your prospects, and doing this will earn you a level of respect and trust you couldn't attain otherwise. Start thinking about who your prospects probably turn to for help and advice. The first people who come to my mind are lawyers, accountants, and bankers.

The stereotype of the typical salesperson is alive and well, and if you fall into the trap of becoming that stereotype, it's extremely difficult to gain the respect of your prospects and to be taken seriously. I remember arguing with managers who suggested that I dress down for appointments and start wearing golf shirts and khakis in order to make my prospects feel more comfortable.

The effects of image are powerful and far-reaching. Look at how people take the advice of doctors without question, when that advice is frequently to undergo painful and often risky surgery. Look at how lawyers work hard to maintain an image of power. I actually know people who worked for one of the major commercial leasing companies. They were required to wear clothes and drive luxury cars they couldn't really afford starting out, but the effects of doing these things were so powerful that their income quickly bridged the gap.

Your image is very important and plays a major role in the level of respect and trust you will get from your prospects. This applies in all areas—your clothes, your grooming, your body language, your accessories such as your briefcase, and how clean your car is. People make all kinds of subconscious judgments about others based on these things, and they can make or break a sale.

# 4

## THINK LIKE A BUSINESS OWNER

### KNOW WHAT'S IMPORTANT TO PROSPECTS

One of the big failures of traditional sales training is that it doesn't teach salespeople how to think like a business owner, and thinking like a business owner is essential to success in sales. In fact, if you can't think in terms of a business owner's needs and wants, you can't speak their language at all.

There are only three things any business owner or executive wants to accomplish: to increase revenues, decrease expenses, and/or increase efficiency (profitability). That's it. You're wasting your time if you're trying to use any other reasons to convince a business owner or executive to buy from you.

While a lot of other things might come to mind, such as decreasing employee turnover, decreasing refund rates, increasing customer loyalty, and so on, all fall under one of the three main categories of business goals.

In order to accomplish this, you need to look at your product and forget about features, how great your company is, and all the other things we have a habit of talking about that really don't matter. A flashy new feature on a piece of equipment isn't going to get their attention unless you can show how it will increase efficiency and therefore profitability.

I didn't realize how much of a problem this really is until I became a business owner myself. I found myself getting annoyed at salespeople who tried to sell something based on features. Conversely, I found myself giving my undivided attention to salespeople who were able to communicate to me, up front, that what they were offering could help me make more money. That's it. Sure, there are gadgets I'd love to have, but every time I'm tempted to buy one, I think to myself, "This won't make money," and I quickly drop the idea.

## PROFIT JUSTIFICATION

This concept is usually known as cost justification, but I like profit justification better. That's because it's much easier to sell something based on the fact that it will turn a profit instead of the idea that it will pay for itself over time.

Accomplishing this requires a very different fact-finding approach than the usual questions asked in appointments. We go into specifics in a later chapter, but for now, realize that your purpose is to gain an understanding of how your product or service will specifically increase profitability, increase revenues, and/or decrease expenses.

Too many salespeople sell on price. This is great if the prospect's goal is to cut costs and you happen to be the low-cost provider. If that's the case, by all means sell on price. However, that's not usually the case. For most of my sales career, I was with the highest-cost provider, and my job day in and day out was to profit-justify my solutions. Keep in mind that a business owner will happily increase expenses if it results in an associated increase in revenues and/or profitability. I do it all the time. I remember a conversation with a marketing consultant who was analyzing my data and looking for ways to cut costs. His conversation kept coming back to reducing costs, and I had to keep reminding him that I actually wanted to increase costs! In other words, because the data showed that every dollar spent on marketing resulted in about four dollars of profit, I wanted to spend as many dollars as possible in order to keep getting four dollars back! With that in mind, don't be bashful about your pricing. If you can profit-justify your offerings, you can be twice as expensive as your nearest competitor and still win the sale.

The chapters on fact finding and the appointment and proposal process go into detail as to how to do this. For now, start thinking about these ideas and the concept of always basing your sales upon those three key points: increasing revenues, decreasing expenses, and/or increasing efficiency and therefore profitability. Get away from the idea of selling on features or your company's reputation.

## AVOID EMPTY RAPPORT BUILDING

A big mistake I see salespeople make is the effort at building rapport. Most sales training advocates building rapport with a prospect in order to break the ice. The usual advice is to do a quick scan of the prospect's office, find something of interest, and comment on it. This might be an award, a piece of sports memorabilia, or something representative of a hobby.

The problem with this is twofold. First of all, decision makers consider their time to be their most precious asset (as you should, too). We've already touched upon the fact that nothing irritates a busy executive more than a waste of time. They've dealt with enough salespeople to know very well that your attempt at building rapport is phony and is totally irrelevant to your purpose for being there. You lose respect and credibility by doing it.

The second and larger problem with attempting to build phony rapport is that it ruins the credibility you've established by inducing the prospect to call you. The next chapter deals more specifically with the psychology behind this, but remember that in order to be supremely successful at selling, you must always present yourself as an authority figure to whom prospects feel they can trust and turn to for advice. By launching into frivolous conversation just for the sake of conversation, you damage that trust. Stick with your real reason for being there.

Rapport is important, but the type of rapport you need to build in order to be successful is professional rapport, not personal. This means knowing your stuff, knowing your prospect's business before you get there, sticking to what's important, being extremely professional, and always underpromising and overdelivering. I was always afraid to underpromise for a long time. However, once I started doing so, prospects had an immensely higher level of trust in me and remained far more loyal. They're automatically suspicious of anyone who overpromises, and it therefore destroys professional rapport. Don't do it.

## WHAT ARE YOUR GOALS?

The single biggest conflict of interest I've seen between salespeople and decision makers is the simple fact that most salespeople think like employees, while most decision makers think like business owners. There are obvious exceptions, such as independent professionals who must sell themselves to obtain clients, but such exceptions are few.

In order to avoid making this kind of mistake with a prospect, you must have a basic working knowledge of how businesses operate and of business finance. I don't mean you should run out and take an accounting class. What I do mean is that you need to understand some basics in order to avoid looking foolish in front of a business owner.

Here's a perfect example of what I'm talking about: One of the most common things I hear salespeople say to business owners is, "Remember, the purchase price or monthly payments are usually tax-deductible and are a write-off to your business." In fact, this is an extremely common comeback to price objections. It makes logical sense to most salespeople, but to a business owner, you've just made yourself look like an idiot and therefore are disqualified from making any recommendations whatsoever. The reason is simply because almost all business expenses are tax deductible. Businesses pay taxes only on profits that are left over after all the bills are paid! To a business owner, an expense is an expense, period.

I didn't realize how many things salespeople say that make them appear entirely unqualified to meet with a business owner until I became a business owner myself. In fact, when salespeople hit me with that line about how their price tag is really a write-off, it ticks me off more than anything any salesperson has ever done. Do yourself a favor and take the time to gain a basic understanding of business finance and accounting so you don't make these mistakes and lose credibility. Chances are you'll be the only salesperson among all of your competitors who have this knowledge, and you'll win far more sales as a result.

# 5

---

# A SHIFT IN POWER

## ATTAINING UNSTOPPABLE CONFIDENCE

One of the inherent flaws in the minds of nearly all salespeople is something resembling an inferiority complex. In some cases it really is an inferiority complex, but it's usually not that severe. However, it's almost always present, unless you're dealing with someone who routinely attains 200 percent of quota and above. Incidentally, the fact that these people are overconfident has a lot to do with their outstanding production.

As for me, the early days of having doors slammed in my face and being hung up on and rudely blown off by prospects had a lasting effect on my confidence, and it took time to overcome that. Instead of becoming immune to rejection like I was told I naturally would, I became increasingly sensitive to it, and the condition known as call reluctance began to set it. I dreaded facing prospects and remember being completely unable to even pick up the phone or visit with prospects in person. The longer this went on, the more my fear was communicated to prospects in subtle ways, and the more I was rejected. It was a vicious circle that many of us have experienced.

I continued to view prospects as superiors. After all, that's what everyone else did, and that seemed to be the message in the training I had received. All day long I heard salespeople saying things such as, "I'll do whatever it takes to earn your business," and almost every trainer taught me to build phony rapport when meeting a new prospect. Look at the prospect's office walls and compliment anything of note, they told me. However, the more I tried to do these things, the more disrespectful, and sometimes even sadistic, my prospects became. At times it turned into a game where they tried to see how much they could get from me without buying anything. I know so many salespeople who routinely buy lunch and rounds of golf for prospects who never buy, and I was guilty of this myself for a while.

My shift away from this state into a condition of supreme confidence began slowly but surely when I started to pay attention to the way I dressed. As a student of Napoleon Hill's works, I came upon some of his writings on the subject, and realized that using the psychology of good clothes was one way to overcome my problem and begin to gain a higher level of respect. I not only began to dress well, but took it to an extreme. I complemented my new wardrobe with an expensive-looking fountain pen and leather-bound notebooks. The effect was profound. Prospects immediately began to pay more attention and listen to me, instead of giving me a gruff, "What do you have?" and demanding the lowest price.

Over time I realized that the clothes themselves had little to do with it. I learned and realized that the change was largely due to the effect those clothes and accessories had on me, and was not necessarily due to the effect they had on my prospects. Whenever I took the advice of "dress like your prospects," which at the time usually meant polo shirts, I never received much respect or undivided attention from prospects. However, when I dressed up, or, in other words, dressed like the people my prospects turned to for advice, I was very confident, and the end result was that affluent prospects took me seriously and showed me a level of respect I hadn't experienced before. I realize now that this was due to the effect that dressing well had on my own mind and not on my prospects' minds.

I bring this up because of what I briefly mentioned in the preface. Cold calling a prospect sets a precedent for a sales process that places the salesperson in a position of need, and places the prospect in the powerful position of one who can fulfill that need. Any of us who have worked with sadistic prospects have experienced this to an extreme. On the other hand, inducing a prospect to call you through a well-managed self-marketing program sets an entirely different precedent. Go back and read the example in Chapter 2 of the process of "buying" as I define it, and how the prospect's frame of mind is set the very moment he or she calls you. They are obviously in need of something, and you are now in the position to provide for that need. You not only look like someone they might turn to for advice; they really ARE turning to you for advice!

Think, for a moment, about the immense advantage you have when you're in a competitive situation and you've successfully created this image and are in a position of power with the prospect. All of your competitors got there through traditional means and are conducting the sales process from a position of need and supplication. They are seen as pests who keep calling, yet you are seen as someone who can actually help. After all, that must be the case if they called you first. Who do you think will get the sale? Can you see why price and other objections suddenly become trivial? Most objections, after all, aren't really objections. They're excuses from people who haven't the courage to say no.

This is very, very important to understand, because once you're in that position of power, it's easy to lose it if you do not carry this persona all the way through to the very end of the sale and beyond. This is why, even after I figured out how to get prospects to call me instead of having to cold call them, I was still losing more sales than I should have. I was conducting appointments and asking questions like, "What will it take to earn your business?" Can you see how that question definitely does not fit into a sales situation where a prospect called you first and sees you as someone whom they are looking to for advice?

As if it isn't bad enough to say things like that in a sales appointment, it's even worse when you've successfully marketed to a prospect and induced them to call you. While that kind of talk is expected from a cold caller, it's very discrediting to someone who is initially seen as a problem solver. It puts you right back into the position of being the one who is in need and who is trying to get something from the prospect, not the other way around.

Early on, when I first managed to stop cold calling and was successfully getting prospects to call me, I did what most other salespeople do when they get a call-in lead. I immediately returned the call, agreed to drop whatever I was doing, and drive to the prospect's office right then and there. This isn't very encouraging to someone in whom you're trying to inspire confidence. Think back to some of the examples of people who are routinely turned to for advice. If you called an attorney for the purpose of setting an appointment, and that attorney said, "I'll come over right now," wouldn't you be at least a little suspicious of that person's credentials? Shouldn't a lawyer have court or appointments with other clients? After all, aren't successful, prosperous people supposed to be busy? Of course they are. I wouldn't put my legal affairs in the hands of a lawyer who has nothing else to do. Nor will prospects be very enthusiastic about entrusting their business to someone who seems to have nothing going on and is available to come by at the drop of a hat. They're not going to trust you to fulfill their needs if you don't at least appear to have a full schedule with other prospects. This isn't too different from the reasons I gave as to why cold calling destroys your status as a business equal; it creates the impression that you have nothing important happening and spend all your time trying to scrape up business.

When I figured this out, even when I really didn't have anything of much importance going on, I started to relax a bit and take my time. My new rule was to return morning calls in the late afternoon and afternoon calls the following morning. That way, I wasn't waiting so long as to be disrespectful but just long enough to create the impression that I was a busy person with lots to do and a perceived waiting list to become my customer.

We've all heard the term "feast or famine," and we all know it to be true. When we get into a slump, it's usually a nasty one, and the more we do to try to get out of it, the worse it gets. On the other hand, when we're on a roll, it looks like it will never end. I remember months when I was already over quota, and had so much more on the table that I couldn't even get to them all. Sooner or later I was back in a slump and getting out of it seemed impossible.

This happens simply because of all the subtle communication that goes on between us and our prospects. Studies have shown that what we say accounts for only 7 percent of our communication. Ninety-three percent consists of body language, vocal tone and inflection, facial expressions, posture, and a host of other subtle communication we don't even know we're capable of. Isn't it true that regardless of whether you're in a feast or famine mode, you don't really change what you say? You're still carrying out the same sales process, asking the same questions, and giving the same presentation. Yet that 93 percent of nonverbal communication is telling the real story. When you get into a slump, it comes across loud and clear and successfully turns off otherwise great prospects. They can sense your desperation and lack of success, and it turns them off. And when you're on a roll, that nonverbal communication literally screams prosperity and draws even more success to you like a magnet. Prospects get a gut feeling that they should go with you, and they do.

Since what we say accounts for only 7 percent and all the rest accounts for 93 percent, it's almost reasonable to round that 93 percent up to 100 percent and round the 7 percent down to 0 and conclude that our nonverbal communication is everything.

It may sound a little farfetched, but I've seen too many real-life examples to doubt it. I remember one salesperson I worked with who went to training, stayed out late every night partying, and napped through class every day. He had learned nothing about any of our products by the time we were out in the field selling. And despite that, his nonverbal communication was so powerfully compelling that he usually outsold everyone else. He didn't know what he was talking about, but that was only 7 percent, and prospects responded to that other 93 percent and bought from him.

I'm not saying product knowledge isn't important. It is. You need to know your product as well as your competitors'. However, realize that even if you're the hands-down expert, if your nonverbal communication is negative, you're not going to succeed no matter how good your selling skills are.

One of the most important ideas you need to understand to become supremely successful at selling is twofold: One, you must be very confident, to a level that almost borders on mild arrogance. Two, you must get into the habit of qualifying prospects OUT instead of merely qualifying them. It's taking things to the next level from the viewpoint of how much respect you'll get from your prospects. The idea of taking the lead and qualifying prospects out is scary at first, and as a result most salespeople are afraid to do it. But if you do, it will save you lots of otherwise wasted time with prospects who aren't really serious and will free that time up for prospects who are actually going to buy.

Don't always be too available. Communicate to your prospects and customers that while you respect them and intend to excel for them, you're busy and important and have a lot on your plate. When someone requests a meeting with you, never say, "Whatever is best for you," even if it's that one big prospect you've been after for months. Offer a choice of dates and times, and create the impression that you are in demand.

## OVERCOMING LIMITING BELIEFS

Although the lack of confidence I experienced early on and the call reluctance that resulted were largely the product of day after day of cold calling with poor results, for most of us, low confidence has much deeper roots and is ingrained in our minds as the result of self-imposed limiting beliefs.

I refer to this as your "inner game." I call the actual sales techniques your "outer game" and firmly believe that you cannot be fully effective with your outer game until you have your inner game in order.

Think about examples of limiting beliefs that you, or people in general, may have. When I was experiencing failure after failure that led to an inability to get any results at all, I was inadvertently using the principle of autosuggestion against me. Autosuggestion is the simple principle that anything you repeat to yourself often enough becomes real in your own mind. The idea that one will eventually believe a lie that is repeated to oneself often enough is really true. In my case, getting up and going to work every day repeating to myself, "This isn't going to work; this will be another day of rejection," is a perfect example of how most salespeople use the principle of autosuggestion in a negative manner. Those ideas took on a life of their own, and eventually became such a powerful force in my mind that I didn't have the drive to do anything productive at all.

Your subconscious mind is always at work. Day and night, while you're awake and especially while you sleep, your subconscious is always working to turn thoughts into reality. The problems begin with the fact that the subconscious has no ability to discern between positive and negative thoughts. It merely works with whatever is fed to it, and translates those thoughts into outward physical action. The subconscious receives and works only with ideas that are passed to it repeatedly, in a spirit of belief. So, because I believed that I would continue to face more rejection, and I repeated that statement to myself often, that's exactly what I got.

Conversely, one may rise to new heights of achievement by deliberately feeding the subconscious mind positive thoughts, repeatedly, in a spirit of belief and in the present tense. For example, if your goal is to become the top salesperson in your company, saying, "I'm going to be the top rep" repeatedly and in a spirit of belief isn't quite enough. You need to say, "I am the top rep. I'm #1 here." Only then can your subconscious mind work to transmute that thought into physical reality.

Let's take a look at two common thoughts that run through the minds of salespeople:

"How can I overcome my fear of rejection?"

"How can I avoid saying the wrong things?"

Let's see how these examples influence your mind negatively and erode your self-confidence: "How can I overcome my fear of rejection?" The problem with this question, although few salespeople realize it, is that it directs the mind to focus on the negative qualities of FEAR and REJECTION rather than on positive virtues. Keep in mind that any thoughts that reach the subconscious mind are accepted by it, processed, and fed back to the conscious mind in the form of outward physical action.

By feeding thoughts of fear and rejection to the subconscious mind, the subconscious sends back to the conscious mind instructions on how to feel even more fear and rejection, and as a result the cycle worsens.

"How can I avoid saying the wrong things?" This one is obvious. By constantly sending thoughts of saying the wrong things to your subconscious, guess what happens? You do exactly that—say the wrong things!

## REFRAMING LIMITING BELIEFS

In order to avoid the damage of limiting beliefs, you must reframe them in a positive light. It isn't enough to simply eliminate them, because that isn't entirely possible, and even if you could, it wouldn't reverse the damage that's already been done. In reframing a limiting belief, you find a way to rephrase it in such a way that it actually becomes a positive thought that reaches your subconscious mind in a spirit of belief and results in productive action. Let's reframe those two examples:

"How can I overcome my fear of rejection?" might become "I'm happy to hear no because it gets bad prospects out of my way," or "Who cares what happens? I'm indifferent to the outcome."

"How can I avoid saying the wrong things?" simply becomes, "I always say the right thing in every situation."

To get into the right frame of mind to be successful every day, write out a positive statement about yourself, and repeat it in the morning in a spirit of enthusiasm and belief. Repeat it to yourself before falling asleep at night as well.

It is especially important to feed positive thoughts to your subconscious mind right before you go to sleep at night because your subconscious works hardest while you sleep. The thoughts you think as you fall asleep at night will determine, to a large degree, how you feel when you wake up in the morning and how your entire day will be. When you have a bad day, it's almost certainly because you thought about troubles or worries the night before!

The fact that the subconscious works hardest while you sleep is the reason why so many coaches recommend reviewing your to-do list and your next day's schedule right before bed. It allows that information to be absorbed and processed by your subconscious mind as you sleep, and in many cases you'll wake up in the morning with fresh, new ideas that will help you achieve your goals that day.

In reframing your mind in a positive manner, and to completely eliminate fear of rejection, start thinking about the idea of pursuing your goals without caring about the outcome of each of your individual actions.

### WHAT'S YOUR SECRET EXCUSE?

Most of us have a Secret Excuse that holds us back from achieving a level of supreme self-confidence, the kind of confidence that would rapidly move us forward toward great achievement. I think, for many people, a Secret Excuse is simply a way of making it easier to avoid facing reality, and therefore have an excuse to not work harder on improving ourselves. Secret Excuses can wire themselves so deeply into our minds that we may not even be aware of the negative effects they're having. Over time, it can not only hamper your professional success, but have a negative effect on all of your life.

Secret Excuses vary but they're always imaginary. Someone may think, for example, that they cannot achieve high success because they didn't go to college. Or maybe it's because they're overweight. Or don't come from a rich family.

Stop right now, figure out what your Secret Excuse is, and write it down! Now, see if you can figure out where that Secret Excuse came from. Did something happen in your life that planted this Secret Excuse in your mind? I never finished college. However, I was brought up to believe that it's impossible to become successful without a college degree, and that the lack of a college education meant certain poverty. For a while my lack of a formal education became my Secret Excuse. There was nothing I hated more than meeting someone new and being asked, "Where did you go to school?" However, I reframed it into a challenge that drove me on to great success. Instead of letting it hold me down, I was soon on a mission to prove that my lack of a college education would not be a liability, but that I would actually achieve a degree of success far beyond those around me who were college educated.

When you figure out what your Secret Excuse is, you must immediately begin to reframe it into something that will motivate you and drive you on to high achievement just like I did.

### YOUR PROSPECTS AND CUSTOMERS NEED YOU!

Remember, you're selling something that your prospects need. If that weren't true, you wouldn't be selling it and your company wouldn't stay in business! You are a business equal in that you can provide prospects with something they need. Your ability to fulfill their needs makes you a trusted partner and advisor.

Always remember that reaching prospects through your system of self-marketing puts you in a position of power and authority right from the start. Use the principles in this chapter to build strong self-confidence, and always carry that confident persona through all sales situations and beyond.

As you implement this system and begin to attract prospects to you, you'll notice the difference right away. Always remind yourself that you're an equal, if not a superior. Since you're starting the relationship at least as an equal in the eyes of the prospect, you can say this to yourself with firm belief because it's true. In addition to regarding you as a business equal, many will view you as an authority figure, for example someone they can turn to for advice. Always carry yourself with supreme confidence and live up to this expectation and level of respect, and great sales success will be assured.

# 6

## THE POWER OF LEVERAGE AND THE ADVANTAGE OF SYSTEMS

### LEVERAGE IS MASSIVE POWER

Although I've already made my case as to why cold calling has become useless in our new economy, the biggest flaw with cold calling is that it is a one-to-one relationship and a one-time occurrence that completely fails to employ any leverage whatsoever.

Leverage is the most powerful force anyone can use to get ahead quickly. In order to understand the power of leverage, imagine a big boulder. You must move this boulder, so you throw all your weight against it. You lean into it, push as hard as you can, and nothing happens. You are powerless to move it, and as a result it stays right where it is.

Now imagine you have a long lever with which to move the boulder. You set the center of the lever on a pivot, push one end of it into the dirt underneath the boulder, and push downward on the other end. The force you've generated with leverage is enough to make the boulder easily roll over.

With that same image in mind, imagine a salesperson who has a large quota, no leads, and is expected to attain 100 percent of quota completely on his own. This salesperson must generate leads and then manage to have time to work those leads and get enough sales closed to keep a job for another month. This person is out beating the streets, knocking on as many doors as possible, and is struggling to make at least 50 calls a day. The goal every day is to set appointments by cold calling, and because getting appointments is a goal in itself, a lot of time is wasted meeting with people just because they're willing, not necessarily because they are genuinely interested in buying. It's a race against the clock with poor odds. Time is running out, and the salesperson is losing the race. This is the equivalent of trying to push that massive boulder all by yourself.

Now imagine a salesperson working for the same company and with the exact same quota. Instead of pounding the pavement and dialing for dollars, this salesperson has employed a comprehensive self-marketing program. About a half-dozen different individual systems are at work in the background. Each system works automatically to attract prospects and generate highly qualified leads. Unlike the salesperson in the first example, half of every day isn't wasted cold calling just to meet with unqualified prospects, and as a result all day every day is free to work those qualified leads. Quota is always exceeded without breaking a sweat. This is leverage at work.

Another way to think of a nonleveraged versus a leveraged system of selling is to think of the difference between working hard and working smart. We've all heard the term "Work smart, not hard," and we know that the people who really get ahead in the business world are those who work smart. I think a combination of both is necessary: Work hard but do it smart. Working hard in a nonleveraged fashion will get you nowhere, or at best, you'll work very hard just to survive. This is the typical example of the salesperson who works 12 hour days to barely make quota and stay employed for another month. This is what managers are inadvertently telling you to do when they say that the key to success is to come in early and stay late.

Time management is another matter and beyond the scope of this book. However, keep one thing in mind: Your quota was designed to be attained working a normal, eight-hour workday just like normal businesspeople. If you have to work 10- or 12-hour days just to make quota, you're not working smart. In fact, if you even have to work a full eight-hour day just to make quota, you're still probably not working smart. If you have a full-scale leveraged system of lead generation in place, and it's had time to develop over several months, you should be a top producer without going more than eight hours each day.

Another fine example of exactly what leverage is can be explained as follows. We've all heard that as salespeople, we're essentially in business for ourselves. This is true to a large degree. One of the reasons I chose sales as a career is the fact that I hated the idea of having a fixed income that never changed no matter how well I performed. I've always had an independent, entrepreneurial spirit and a profession in sales allowed me to express that. However, there is much confusion as to the differences between a true business owner and a self-employed business owner. If you own a business but have to work in it, it's not a business system; it's a job. A true business owner owns a system that continues to work regardless of whether the owner works or not. The true business owner quickly gets ahead of the self-employed person because as the system works automatically, the owner is free to do other things to generate income. The self-employed person, on the other hand, is always tied up running the business and therefore has little or no free time to pursue other opportunities.

It's exactly the same in sales. If you are working in a nonleveraged fashion, getting up every day and making your 50 calls, or finishing out a good month with an empty funnel and having to start all over again, you're like the self-employed person. Your income is limited because a significant portion of your time must be devoted to prospecting for new business. You ARE the system, and if you don't work, nothing happens. A salesperson who uses a leveraged system of self-marketing, by contrast, need not spend time prospecting. The leads will come in automatically. This is the same as the true business owner who makes money regardless of whether or not he chooses to work each day.

Granted, you still need to spend the time to work the leads your system generates. However, a huge amount of time is saved, you'll have leads coming in consistently, and your income will go up dramatically as a result.

You must remember that as salespeople, we're only paid to make sales. We're not paid for time spent cold calling. We're not paid for time spent writing proposals and meeting with prospective customers. We're not paid for driving in our car. We're paid to make sales, so think of how much higher your income would be if you spend all your time making sales. For example, let's say you currently spend half your time on cold calling and the other half on selling. If you could effectively recover that time you spend on cold calling and use it to close sales, you've doubled your income. From my experience, and in my years of selling, the time spent prospecting was more than half. Especially when I was just starting out, I easily spent four-fifths of each day cold calling. So, in that example, if I could recover that four-fifths of each day spent cold calling and convert it to time spent making sales, I'd multiply my income by five.

The other big aspect of leverage that it effectively multiplies the number of people you can contact in a given day. A salesperson who cold calls can call only one person at a time. Some form of leveraged marketing, however, can effectively contact dozens of people at a time. Consider a web site. Thousands of people may be on a web site at the same time. But if that same company decided to get rid of the site and have a salesperson make calls instead, only one person at a time could be contacted. The other part of the equation is obvious: People who visit the site do so willingly and have some degree of interest. People you cold call are usually not at all interested in what you have to offer.

## THE ADVANTAGE OF SYSTEMS AND A SYSTEM OF SYSTEMS

A system, as we've just seen, is something that's set up to run on its own without the need for active participation from its owner. There's work involved in building a system, but once it's up and running, it continues to work automatically.

Everything is based on systems. There is the example of an automobile, and the example of an aircraft. Your company is a system. A sales department is a system. Your office is a system. Even your job is a system. To your company, your position is a system, the purpose of which is to generate revenue for the company. The key is whether you build systems to work on your behalf, or if you yourself are the system.

Within your position, various micro-systems exist to carry out the overall process of selling. There's prospecting or lead generation. There is the actual sales process, and after that is the follow-up and upsell process. These components work together to build the system that is your job.

Your production is maximized by setting up your systems to work with utmost efficiency. While the sales process itself is hands-on, you can automate the lead-generation process. Once it's up and running, it will really be a system of systems. You'll learn about the individual marketing methods you can employ to ultimately build your self-marketing system. The ultimate goal of your system, of course, is to generate qualified leads on a consistent basis so you won't have to, and to do so automatically without tying up your productive selling time.

# Part Two

---

# Your Self-Marketing System for Lead Generation

# 7

# SELF-MARKETING BASICS

### WHAT IS SELF-MARKETING?

Self-marketing is a marketing campaign that you build in order to generate a consistent supply of qualified leads. This is no different from a regular marketing campaign that might be executed by a large company; however, it's scaled down to be practical and effective for one salesperson—you.

The problem that we all face is that we either work for a company that provides no marketing support, or we work for ourselves and are on our own when it comes to generating leads. The only two options, then, are to cold call, or to conduct a marketing campaign. We've already established the fact that cold calling no longer produces satisfactory results, and because a full-scale marketing campaign is prohibitively expensive, we have little choice but to carry out a well-organized self-marketing effort.

The most important aspect of a self-marketing system is leverage. If you're out there trying to find leads on your own, you have no leverage. It's you and only you, and because there's only one of you, your leverage factor is one. A self-marketing system, on the other hand, can easily multiply that factor to such a degree that you have a plentiful supply of leads coming to you on a consistent basis. If you build a system that generates as many leads as four salespeople could by cold calling, you're operating with a leverage factor of four. If your system generates as many as nine salespeople could, your leverage factor is nine, and so on.

Go back to the examples of systems and think about the jet aircraft. Forget about the mechanical systems for a moment and think of the system of people working on and around the plane in order to carry out each flight. At a minimum, there is a pilot and copilot, flight attendants, baggage handlers, the foodservice staff, fuelers, maintenance people, the driver of the truck that pushes the plane back, and so on. Now think about what it would take for only one person to make all this happen. The pilot would have to land, open the door, and make sure everyone exits safely. Then he would have to get out, unload the baggage and load it onto the carts, load the baggage for the next flight, refuel the plane, do a maintenance check and make any needed repairs, get back on the plane, run through the cabin and clean up, unload all the garbage, load the new supply of food and drinks for the next flight, get the passengers for the next flight boarded safely, jump back out and drive the truck to push the plane back from the gate, climb back in, lock the door, and fly off. Then he'd have to put the plane on autopilot several times during flight in order to attend to passengers' needs and carry out the food and beverage service.

This sounds crazy, and it is, but it's no different from what one salesperson is trying to do by operating without leverage and conducting all sales activities one-on-one and without the help of systems. If you're trying to do all of your own prospecting, appointments, proposals, follow-up calls, more appointments, paperwork, order entry, meetings, reports, training, and more, you're no different from the pilot who tries to operate an entire plane all alone. There's a slim chance you'll succeed, but even if you do, you'll be overworked and will never do as good a job as you could with the help of systems.

Another thing that systems accomplish is leveraging you to be competitive in today's economy. The biggest difference between the Industrial Age and the Information Age, as far as the sales profession is concerned, is the simple fact that prospects have less need for salespeople as time goes on. They don't need to speak with us on the phone or in person when most or all of the information we can provide is readily available at their fingertips. In the Industrial Age, it was important to be in the right place at the right time. In the Information Age, if we expect to succeed, we must be in all places at all times. Your message must reach prospects in a variety of ways and at a variety of times. It goes back to the discussion on why cold calling doesn't work because it makes timing work against you rather than for you. By using leveraged systems to figuratively be in all places at all times, you defeat the element of timing right from the start and put yourself in a position to win.

## CREATING YOUR MESSAGE

Before you can build your marketing system, you first need to figure out what your message will be. After all, the sole purpose of marketing is to get your message in front of qualified prospects and give them an incentive to contact you. Therefore, the content of your message is of supreme importance. No matter how well your marketing system is planned and executed, if the message isn't effective, you won't get results.

The key is to create a message that pushes a decision maker's buttons. This means thinking like a business owner, not like a salesperson. We tend to think of the outward features and advantages of our products or services. A business owner is concerned only about how it will achieve one of the three business goals: increase revenues, decrease expenses, or increase efficiency/profitability. So, what you need to do first is figure out and understand how whatever it is you're offering can accomplish one or more of these business goals.

To really achieve a powerful, targeted message, start thinking in terms of what kind of headline might catch your prospects' attention. This headline must be related to the three chief goals of a business executive. Think of all the different ways your product can increase revenues, decrease expenses, and increase efficiency/profitability. Now start writing down a list of every possible headline you can use to get a decision maker's attention. Take your time. You don't have to do this all at once. It can even be something you keep with you in a notebook. Keep it handy at all times since more and better ideas will come to you as you brainstorm and think about it.

## WHAT YOU MUST COMMUNICATE TO PROSPECTS

Once you have your list of headlines, you need to figure out exactly how you'll communicate those messages in a way that will get prospects' attention. Remember, your headlines won't always necessarily be used as literal headlines, although several forms of self-marketing will use them as such. The real purpose of headlines is to give you a clear, concise message that you'll communicate to prospects in a variety of ways. The entire purpose of narrowing them down to brief headlines is to give you a direct message to work with, rather than something too verbose and tedious that will not grab your prospects' attention. Also keep in mind that you won't simply choose one and stick with that as your key message. If you have a list of several headlines, you'll eventually want to use all of them, then gradually weed out the less effective ones and focus your efforts on the most effective ones.

Always keep in mind that in self-marketing, your purpose is to gain the prospect's interest without cold calling. In order to do this, your message must be powerful enough to get the prospect to contact you or give the okay to receive further communication from you. With that in mind, there are several key points to remember when crafting your message.

First of all your message must offer something to the prospect that they couldn't otherwise get; you must make it clear that they can't lose by contacting you. One good example is what I used when I was running a telecom sales agency. The typical sales pitch in telecom is something along the lines of, "Save money on your phone bill." This is an old message that doesn't work anymore, so I built a campaign with the headline, "High-Speed Internet Available Everywhere!" Since getting high-speed Internet service was a challenge at the time, the phones rang and we sold tons without cold calling. In fact, telecom companies almost universally require their sales reps to conduct a two-appointment sales process. However, the leads my campaign generated were so qualified that we never even met with 70 percent of the prospects; they agreed to buy over the phone and we simply faxed the paperwork for them to sign! (By the way, that campaign took place about three years before the time of this writing and I continue to get calls today.) To put it simply, offer them something outstanding.

Another important thing to keep in mind is that you must target the right people. One of the biggest mistakes salespeople make is addressing something to the "owner" or "manager." The problem with doing this is that your marketing piece is immediately written off as junk and discarded. If you do not have a targeted name, it's better to use no name at all than to use a generic one like those I mentioned. Even though having the correct contact name is the best possible scenario, having no name is better than having a generic title.

You must also creatively focus on what your prospects want. To do so you should brainstorm over a period of days and come up with an extensive list of headlines that quickly tell prospects that you can help them achieve one of the principal business goals. Although you'll use some of those actual headlines as such, the real point of this is so that you know, in your mind, exactly how your products and services can help. I'm not talking about an Initial Benefit Statement. That's a salesy way to go about it, and it sparks instant sales resistance in your prospect. I'm talking about how to communicate directly to the prospect that what you are offering will enable them to achieve their goals. Not only will this enable you to create powerful marketing materials, but it will make you a far more effective salesperson in your regular verbal and written communications. One of my problems early on in sales was that I was too verbose and talked entirely too much instead of being direct and to-the-point, which is what works best with a qualified prospect.

Keep this in mind: You must always remember our definitions of buying and selling, and always work from the mindset of inducing prospects to buy from you, instead of your having to sell to them. This will help you avoid the common trap of trying to push what you're selling instead of giving them what they want. Apply the concept of always giving them what they want. It's the only sure way to have qualified prospects contacting you on a consistent basis. A great example of this goes back to my telecom days. One of the biggest challenges facing telecom salespeople is the fact that, thanks to a lot of disreputable companies in that industry, telecom salespeople have gained an unfair reputation of being pushy and dishonest (telecom is notorious for overpromising and underdelivering). Much like the fear of pushy salespeople that makes some of us avoid car dealerships, a lot of telecom prospects try to avoid the sales process and as a result never buy services that would legitimately help them. So, with that in mind, I added the following headline to our marketing pieces: "Don't Deal with Pushy Telecom Salespeople—Call Us Instead!" Guess what? Prospects did just that. They called us. The obvious irony here is that we were telecom salespeople! But by neutralizing the biggest cause of prospects' resistance right up front, we closed a lot of easy, noncompetitive, high-margin sales.

While you're working on your outward image, you must also name yourself or your product. I'm not talking about your actual name. I'm talking about titling yourself in a way that connects with prospects. For example, if you're selling widgets, your marketing materials may name you as "Your personal widget expert." Again, you must offer the prospects something outstanding, and you must form their opinion of you. Don't leave anything to chance and let them form an opinion. You might also be "Your certified expert on widgets." Whatever you come up with, it must stand out from the crowd, it must suggest that you are the utmost authority, and you must include something that suggests exclusivity. The word "your" does this best.

While we're on the subject of creating your message, please don't include generic information about your company. You must especially avoid anything that comes off as bragging. An example is something I've seen big companies do. They'll drop names of big clients or mention that they have several Fortune 500 clients. As soon as you do that, smaller prospects assume they'll be treated like a number and will be taken care of only after the big customers are.

The goal of a marketing message is to get the prospect to respond. You must motivate them to get into action, and you must make it quick and easy for them to reply. Use something that creates a sense of urgency. Limited-Time Offer is common but it's so overused, even when it's not true, that a lot of prospects won't believe it. It does work, though, if you tie it into something else. "Free Installation until June 30" is an example of a limited-time offer that is considered legitimate because it's specific. The point is to give them a reason to call you now instead of putting your information into a file folder. In fact, using the words "right now" are more effective than you might imagine! I've seen increased response rates from marketing pieces that included the words "right now" as part of the call to action. Be sure to make it easy for them to respond. At a minimum, you want to include your phone number (preferably a cell number), your e-mail address, your web site address, and a fax-back form if it's a printed marketing piece. A fax-back form is nothing more than a few fill-in-the-blank lines such as name and phone number that prospects fill out and fax back to you. For some reason, the response rates with fax-back forms are at least three times higher than with marketing pieces including only your phone number and expecting prospects to call you. It's a quick and effective way to multiply response rates from any type of printed marketing material.

Remember to be creative, offer them something outstanding, focus on what they really want, form an opinion of yourself for them, give yourself a powerful name, and include a strong call to action.

# 8

---

# A TWIST ON COLD CALLING

### COLD CALLS ARE A FLEETING MOMENT IN TIME

One of my biggest frustrations with cold calling is that a cold call isn't tangible. It's a one-time event. It happens, and if you don't get an appointment or make a sale, it's over and that's it. Sure, I usually got a contact name, but it was difficult to reach those people when they knew that my call was a cold call. In fact, I found that leaving my business card behind made things even worse. This guaranteed that the decision maker would know who I was and therefore would avoid my call.

It bothered me that cold calls were gone in an instant. It especially bothered me knowing how many hours each day I was devoting to cold calling with no cumulative results. I began thinking of ways to take some form of constructive action on cold calls that would open the door for the possibility of a sale down the road. I didn't want to leave a faceless business card; I wanted prospects to know exactly what I had to offer and how it would help them in order to motivate them to pick up the phone and contact me.

After some experimentation, I settled on a simple, one-page flyer. Nothing fancy. To my amazement, the response was nothing short of fabulous, and I was getting it with far less effort than I was previously expending on cold calling with dismal results!

---

The idea came to me due to earlier successes I'd achieved through the use of targeted mail. Once I'd perfected the piece I was using, I began thinking about the challenge of getting the mail opened. I came up with some very clever and effective techniques that I explain in a subsequent chapter, but I still wanted everyone to open and read my mail, not just some people. I decided to try handing them out door-to-door, and I was stunned by the volume of qualified leads that resulted.

Because the transition from cold calling to self-marketing is such a drastic change for most salespeople, and because self-marketing efforts are cumulative, I recommend flyer distribution as a first step. This is because it's something you can do to supplement your current prospecting efforts, and it has the most cumulative results out of all the techniques I teach, so you'll experience increasing returns over time. Best of all, it costs little or nothing, and if you're on a tight budget, it's the perfect way to begin realizing increased sales and increased commissions, and as a result will provide you with seed money to begin working on other self-marketing tactics that might require a small investment.

## CREATING YOUR MARKETING PIECE

One of the most important aspects of a simple, effective one-page flyer is the fact that it must capture the prospect's attention without looking like junk mail. It must be very clean and simple, but at the same time it must pique the prospect's interest in achieving one of the three major business goals.

I've found that the most effective layout for a powerful flyer is as follows:

### *Headline*

The headline is the most important element. The good news is that once you spend time brainstorming, you'll have lots of great headlines. As I mentioned, I recommend that you narrow your list down to the best ones and try using all of them. Over time you'll begin to see which ones are producing the best results and which ones can be discarded.

Remember, the key to an effective headline is that it must address one of the three main business goals. As an example, I share with you the headline from my very first flyer when I was selling telephone systems. The headline read, "Free Installation on All New Phone Systems This Month!" Just to the left of the headline was a cartoon depicting a boardroom meeting with one empty seat. The caption read, "If you don't have voice mail, someone isn't getting the message." This text/cartoon headline addressed the major business goals as such:

- The text "Free Installation on All New Phone Systems This Month!" addressed the business goal of decreasing expenses.
- The cartoon addressed the business goal of increasing efficiency.

Think about ways you can supplement your set of headlines like I did with that cartoon. There are dozens of web sites that can provide you with similar cartoons or clip art at little or no cost, and that will substantially improve your flyer's effectiveness and response rates.

### First Paragraph of Body Text

Here you want to include a few sentences building on benefits announced in your headline. I prefer to keep it short and simple, and to give it an easy-to-read look; nobody is going to read a paragraph that looks long and tedious. Just a few sentences, at 14- or 16-point text on a standard letter sized sheet of paper is ideal. On my phone system flyer, the opening body text was:

> We're now offering free installation on all new telephone systems purchased before the end of the month, including competitive lease rates! We also offer value-added solutions such as voice mail and multi-site networking that can drastically improve your productivity.

This paragraph, like the headline, touches on the business goal of decreasing expenses through free installation, and also revisits the increased efficiency theme through its mention of value-added services that can improve productivity. It also added slightly more detail than the headline by mentioning competitive lease rates (which can decrease the prospect's expenses) as well as another example of value-added services in addition to voice mail (which can improve the prospect's efficiency).

Remember, this paragraph must have a clean look that will compel prospects to read it right away.

### *Bullet Points Describing Key Benefits*

Here I like to list two or three bullet points detailing key points about the product that would be of interest to a prospect. What I like to accomplish here is to increase the potential audience. In other words, address common objections that prospects might have. For example, when I was selling phone systems, I had to make sure that smaller businesses weren't alienated by the fact that I was representing a large company that had very large clients. I also had to be sure to alleviate any potential objections that might be raised as a result of my headline or body text. Here are the bullet points that were included in my first phone system flyer:

- Systems available from two phones to thousands.
- Flexible leasing options, even for brand-new companies.
- Installation can be rolled into your monthly payment.

As you can see, I immediately eliminated the possibility that smaller companies would not call for fear that they might be too small to work with the big company I represented. I also addressed concerns about financing that all startup companies have, and finally I addressed a common concern about being hit with a whopping installation bill despite the fact that the equipment itself may be leased.

### *Brief Closing Paragraph and "Call to Action"*

This is where you motivate the prospect to contact you. It simply consists of one or two closing sentences describing what the prospect will miss out on by not calling you, followed with a call to action. Mine read as follows: "Don't miss out on this limited-time free installation offer and our exclusive rock-bottom lease rates. Call me right now or complete and fax the following form." The first sentence reminds the prospect that the free installation offer is for a limited time only, and reminds them again of the highly competitive financing rates available only from my company. The next sentence tells them to either call me or to send in the fax-back form located on the bottom of the flyer.

### *Contact Information and Fax-Back Form*

This one is self-explanatory; you simply include your contact information as well as a fax-back form. The fax-back form is essential here; in tracking results from my own flyers, I found that my response rate tripled with a fax-back form! For some reason, prospects who are reluctant to pick up the phone will readily fax you the form. The best part about this is that you can use it to gauge which flyers are getting the best response. Since prospects have to fax the entire page back, you know right away which flyer they've responded to! This becomes essential as you track results and determine what works and what doesn't. Use a private fax number, either one that goes to a fax machine in your home or a virtual fax service that comes to your e-mail. It's unpleasant to mention but there are sticky fingers in many offices and you don't want someone else taking your leads.

Your contact information should contain the essentials such as your cell number, e-mail address, and web address. When I mention a web address, hopefully it will be your personal web address rather than your company's. You learn how to quickly and inexpensively set up your own personal web site in a later chapter, and why doing so is very effective.

Keep the fax-back form simple. After all, you're just after a name and telephone number. It's simply an additional way to get prospects to contact you. Include blanks for name, company (if this is going out to business prospects), and telephone number. If you're offering a variety of products and services, you may want to include an "I'm interested in" blank. This is especially useful if your product line includes very low-margin products that you'd like to avoid, for example if you're a copier salesperson and someone merely wants to buy a toner cartridge. I began using this in my phone system days after having wasted entirely too much time calling people back who merely needed a new battery for their cordless phone or something equally trivial.

For the physical layout of your flyer, either portrait or landscape is fine. I always preferred landscape because it looked cleaner and was probably read by more prospects. Remember to keep it simple; all you need is something you can run off copies of and distribute to prospects. Tri-fold brochures or multiple colors aren't necessary.

## GETTING YOUR MESSAGE OUT

Obviously, no flyer would be effective unless it gets in front of the people who can act on it! With that in mind, I'd like to discuss some ideas on effective flyer distribution.

As I mentioned earlier, one of the best things about starting a self-marketing program with flyer distribution is the fact that self-marketing results are cumulative and you'll need to keep doing what you're currently doing for a while. If in-person cold calling is part of your current prospecting routine, you can continue doing that but start leaving flyers on every call.

I started out simply. I'd walk through the door, hand my flyer to the receptionist, politely say, "If you can forward this to the appropriate person, that would be great—have a great day," grab a business card if they were out on the front desk, and leave! That's it! I didn't upset anyone, nobody yelled, "No soliciting!," and each visit took only about a minute. If I encountered someone at the front desk who was busy or on the phone, I left my flyer on the desk and smiled, then left. They always accepted it. They appreciated the fact that I wasn't interrupting their busy day. Cold calls interrupt, but dropping off useful information does not. The best part is that I was so happy to have stopped the usual, stressful cold calling routine that I constantly wore a gigantic smile, and that smile was infectious! It was received very favorably by the people I came into contact with, and as a result they happily accepted my flyers and were sure to pass them on to the correct decision makers. It's important to be in a great mood when you're out doing this. Do whatever it takes to get into that mood before you begin your flyer distribution. For me, all it took was the right music in the car.

In order to track my activity, I'd simply run off as many copies each morning as I wanted to distribute, then go at it until they were all gone. One of the great things about this is that you don't wind up counting the wasted ones, for example where someone refuses to take the flyer. It doesn't happen often but it happens. Stick with this method of running off your copies each day and not stopping until they're gone. I found that if I simply kept a supply of flyers in the car and went out each day with the intent of distributing as many as possible, I usually distributed about 20 before quitting, and I never realized how little I was accomplishing this way.

## EMPLOY LEVERAGE: MAKE IT AUTOMATIC

You'll undoubtedly realize tremendous results from your flyer efforts doing it all by yourself. You can expect to at least triple the amount of leads you'd get by cold calling the same number of contacts each day, and on top of that, you can easily double or triple the number of contacts made by using flyers instead of cold calling simply because it doesn't take nearly as much time to complete.

As great as the results from your own personal flyer distribution efforts will be, at some point you'll want to begin applying leverage. Most of us have found pizzeria and restaurant menus hanging on our doorknobs. Guess what? These pieces are distributed by companies that specialize in flyer distribution.

After I increased my commission income back in the phone system days and had some capital on hand to work with, I began coming up with ways to multiply my efforts and employ leverage. I had never heard of flyer distribution companies until I saw an advertisement from one completely by accident. It was—you guessed it—a flyer, dropped off at our office. I called for more information and the pricing was very reasonable. Because they were a division of a printing company, they also handled the copying. Since I had purchased a 5,000-flyer distribution, it was a relief to not have to make that many copies, then lug them all down there.

They put me on their schedule, which was booked for about a month, then finally I received a call that my flyers had started going out. Since I had telephone numbers, my e-mail address, and a fax-back form on the flyer, I was ready and waiting for the leads to start coming in, and they did! Not only did I immediately begin receiving several phone calls a day, at the end of every day I came home and found a stack of leads on the fax machine. I'd have at least three each day and up to six or seven on a good day. My schedule immediately filled up with qualified appointments as the flyer distribution continued and the leads continued to pour in. The best part about having this many leads to work with was the fact that I could be picky about qualifying prospects out, and soon came to the point where I would meet only with prospects who were ready and eager to buy.

Over the next several months, I sold about 50 phone systems thanks to that single flyer distribution campaign. In the end a $300 campaign earned me about $15,000 in commissions.

In locating a flyer distribution company, check your local yellow pages and search online. If you have difficulty locating one, ask pizzerias whom they use. Nearly all of them use flyer distribution services.

Flyer distribution is the quickest and simplest way to get started with self-marketing. As you have seen, you can start small and with no cost, and quickly expand your effort to run automatically and with a tremendous amount of leverage. And this is just the beginning!

# 9

## POWERFUL PHONE TECHNIQUES THAT WORK!

### THE IMAGE OF SUPREME POWER

In order to understand how to powerfully utilize the phone, you must first comprehend the concepts of image and of being perceived as powerful, and how these ideas are communicated over the telephone.

Let's take a look at the typical way the phone is used by salespeople. This method fails to project an image of power: "Hi, this is Frank with DN Advisors, how are you today? I'm calling because we have a new method of selling that can increase your revenues. I'll be in your area next Wednesday—is ten or three o'clock better for you?"

Think about this type of call from the prospect's perspective. Would you be compelled to accept an appointment? Or would your automatic sales resistance go up? Chances are, you'd experience heavy sales resistance, say you're not interested, and hang up the phone.

Now, let's take a look at a call that creates an impression of power. Imagine you're a prospect, and think of how you'd feel. Compare this call with the previous example: "Good morning. I'm an executive assistant with the office of Frank Rumbauskas. I'm pleased to inform you that Mr. Rumbauskas would like to meet with you, and his schedule shows that he has 30 minutes available on Thursday morning at ten. I'll go ahead and pencil you in."

If you're a prospect receiving this call, you immediately assume the person with whom you'll be meeting is important. Chances are, the image of a powerful executive came into your mind when you got this call. You automatically accepted the appointment, because, after all, it must be important if this is how they set up their meetings!

Can you see how effective the second example would be, especially compared to the first example of a typical sales call?

The effective way to use the telephone in prospecting is not to make the calls yourself. In fact, this single difference makes the distinction between cold calling and marketing.

You'll first need to find someone who would be available to make your calls. I suggest starting small and using the money you make as a result to gradually increase the scale of your efforts. A fantastic way to get started, the most common way that I've seen my students use, is to simply find someone who can do this for you in their spare time, for a minimal amount of compensation. Starting out, the best scenario is an arrangement where the person making your calls is paid a flat amount by you for each appointment set, and/or a bonus for every sale made. Typically the person who gets the ball rolling is a spouse, teenage or adult child, or other relative. My students who have realized the biggest success with this had a spouse, a child, or relative who is in high school or college make calls to start.

If you cannot find anyone to do this, or if you are able and willing to spend some money initially, it's fairly easy to find a contract telemarketer to make your calls. This is a better way to go because you'll have a skilled caller working on your behalf, and you will get a lot more appointments as a result.

In the past, I've heard numerous objections to my recommendations as to how to use the phone effectively, so I'd like to address that right now just in case those same thoughts are going through your head. The argument I hear most often is that phone calls are simply another form of cold calling, and if I am against cold calling, why would I recommend a mere variation on cold calling? The reason has to do with the fact that selling and prospecting are entirely different skill sets. Prospecting and selling are usually regarded as being one and the same. In fact, most salespeople consider prospecting to be one of the major steps of a sale. I strongly disagree because great salespeople who can develop and close qualified prospects are usually terrible at prospecting and hate it as a result. On the other hand, those who are great at prospecting and setting appointments usually fall short when it comes to advanced selling tactics, such as needs identification, profit justification, and presenting.

To put it quite simply, prospecting is not selling, and selling is not prospecting. They are different skill sets, and the best results are achieved when prospecting is left to those who do it well and selling is left to true sales professionals. This is why companies that excel in sales performance employ an organized lead-generation effort through a combination of marketing campaigns and telemarketers who specialize in developing leads and setting appointments. The salespeople then receive the leads developed by the telemarketers and close them. So, as you can see, separating sales from prospecting is the most effective overall strategy, and by doing so yourself, you'll begin to attain sales numbers far beyond your previous attainment.

It isn't difficult to find a contract telemarketer or appointment setter to make your calls. These people usually maintain contact with networking groups and can be found simply by asking around within such groups. You can also locate them by searching online. The standard compensation arrangement is usually a small hourly rate, sometimes with a minimum of around 10 hours, plus a small commission for each appointment set that results in a sale. In order to avoid scheduling conflicts, simply keep blocks of time clear and designate those for your appointment setter's use. That way you can avoid scheduling conflicts while your appointment setter is busy developing more leads and filling up those designated blocks of time with fresh, qualified appointments. This is leverage at work!

The next step up from a contract telemarketer is hiring the services of an outbound call center specializing in appointment setting. This isn't nearly as expensive as you may think; in fact, many call centers of this type offer packages starting out as low as a couple of hundred dollars per month. You can find the outbound call centers in your area in the yellow pages and contact them regarding rates and packages, or check their web sites for pricing information. Depending on what's available, you may be better off starting out this way instead of with an independent telemarketer. In either case, you'll eventually want to build your efforts over time to the point where you have a definite need for the services of an outbound call center. The larger your efforts become, the more leverage you have working for you, and the more money you can make with less work on your part.

As to the script your caller will use, that's something best worked on together. Offer examples of what has worked for you in the past. An experienced telemarketer or call center will have scripts they're comfortable with; in this case, it's usually best to have them do what they do best and simply apply it to your particular products. You want to get the most for your money, not to mention the fact that a big part of acquiring leverage and building systems is learning to delegate and avoid micromanaging the people working on your behalf. We all know from personal experience how devastating micromanagement is to sales, so now that you're becoming your own manager of sorts, be careful not to sabotage yourself by micromanaging your people.

The best part of whatever script you decide upon is that when your callers introduce themselves as your executive assistants, they're not lying; they really are your executive assistants! They're helping to do your work for you so your time is free to make money. I say this with the hope that you'll realize just how important you're becoming and how much more success you'll achieve through these efforts. By implementing these strategies, you're establishing your very own business system that will work for you to increase your income. If you think back to the chapter on leverage and the distinction between a business owner and a self-employed person, you're effectively stepping into the role of a true business owner by putting these strategies into action. If you hope to someday own your own company, you're gaining knowledge essential to the attainment of that goal.

In addition to setting appointments, a telemarketer can follow up on other efforts such as direct mail. If you're doing your own flyer distribution, take a card from every office you walk into and give them to your appointment setter to call. Even if he or she calls a prospect who has already called you first, it looks very impressive to have your assistant following up on your leads and will give you that much more of an advantage with that prospect!

# 10

---

# WHY E-MAIL BEATS THE PHONE

### E-MAILS VERSUS PHONE CALLS

The traditional method of making initial contact is over the phone. While some don't think of calling a known decision maker as a cold call, it most definitely is. The following challenges are especially common on the phone:

- You cannot get past the gatekeeper.
- They only take handwritten phone messages; therefore the prospect sees only your name and number and has no idea what the call is about.
- You're constantly faced with evasive tactics such as, "What is this call regarding?"
- You get voice mail, leave a message, but get no return call.
- You reach the prospect, who can't be bothered or is having a bad day, and since your script doesn't prepare you for this, you blow it with that prospect and are locked out of any potential opportunity there.

There are plenty of other scenarios that can take place to defeat your telephone efforts. Voice mail alone poses endless problems, some that many salespeople are completely unaware of. A popular tactic executives use to avoid salespeople is to set up a separate mailbox to which the receptionist sends all sales calls. The catch is that this mailbox is never checked! In other words, your message will never be heard by anyone; talk about a waste of time.

The other big problem with voice mail is the fact that cold calls aren't returned even when they are heard. In my experience, less than 1 call is returned for every 10 messages left.

After a while I began sending polite introductory e-mails to prospects. Nearly everyone has an e-mail address on their cards, and if they don't, you can usually find them on the company's web site. I was astounded at the result. Instead of getting 1 return call for every 10 voice mails left, I was consistently getting 5 or 6 replies for every 10 e-mails I sent! Even the people who weren't interested would reply back with a polite, "We have no needs at this time but we appreciate the information and thank you." I was amazed simply because this was such a contrast from the coldness I always experienced on the phone. It seems backwards, but more warmth and personality came through those e-mails than ever did on the phone.

There are several reasons why prospects will respond to an e-mail while those very same prospects will refuse to take a phone call:

1. It's convenient. It takes only a few seconds to type out a reply. A phone call takes longer and one never knows how long it might last.
2. They know what it's about. Your e-mail explained this, so they don't have to look at a phone message and wonder who is calling and why.
3. It doesn't interrupt their day. Nearly all of us send and receive e-mails while we're doing other things, unlike a phone call, which generally requires us to stop everything else in order to talk and listen.
4. The fear of salespeople is absent. Remember, the people who go to extremes to avoid salespeople are people who fear salespeople and fear being sold. They're afraid to talk on the phone because they don't want to hear a pitch, but e-mail is different. They can take their time in reading and replying to your message, and can type their thoughts out and not have to worry about saying the wrong thing.

5. It's natural. Everybody e-mails friends and family nowadays. Getting a call from a stranger is somewhat unusual but when it comes to e-mail, it's just as familiar as with everyone else.

6. It's not a waste of anyone's time. The number one way to turn off a busy, important person is to do something to waste that person's time. Prospects appreciate the fact that you approached them in such a low-key manner rather than interrupting their day with a phone call.

The bottom line is that e-mail is not annoying and it's more convenient, not to mention the fact that it's becoming the standard method of communication nowadays.

## MAKING INITIAL CONTACT VIA E-MAIL

When I talk about using e-mail for prospecting, I'm not referring to mass e-mailing, or "spamming." I'm referring to a short, polite, personalized e-mail. I always used the same standard cut-and-paste e-mail that I kept on my desktop as a text file. When the time came to contact new prospects, I pasted the same text into each message and simply added the prospect's name to the greeting.

In deciding what you're going to write, think back to the elements of your flyer. Since this is simply another form of written marketing, you'll want to stick with the same guidelines and message. Use all of the same elements but personalize them so they read like a note rather than a sales letter. Also, if you got the person's e-mail address from a business card, it's a good idea to add, "I picked up your card when I was in your office recently."

## FOLLOWING UP VIA E-MAIL

In addition to using e-mail to make initial contacts, I also love e-mail for following up with prospects with whom you've already worked, whether you're still keeping the line of communication open for a potential sale or you've already converted this prospect into a customer and are keeping in touch after the fact.

Just like prospects who see a phone message and have no idea what it's about, many potential prospects with whom you're following up will have no idea why you're calling. As salespeople, we tend to remember every detail of every potential deal that's not yet closed. Prospects, on the other hand, typically don't remember anything and even only a few weeks after a meeting will have no idea who you are. People are busier than ever these days, and catching someone off-guard with a phone call doesn't help. An e-mail, on the other hand, gives them a minute or two to think about it and remember what it's about. They also tend to appreciate e-mails and prefer them over phone calls for the reasons we've already covered.

## EMPLOY LEVERAGE: USING AUTORESPONDER SYSTEMS

An autoresponder is merely an archive of prewritten e-mails that are sent out automatically to prospects at predetermined intervals. In other words, you might have a few brief notes of a few sentences each you'd like to send out to prospects to keep in touch. Since doing this manually would be very time-consuming, automating this task is a great way to become more efficient because the e-mails will always go out and your sales will increase because of the assured ongoing contact.

There are dozens of autoresponder services that you can quickly find by searching online, and the services are very low-cost. I use an autoresponder system in my company today on a large scale, and even that only costs $20 per month. Once you get an account set up, all you have to do is type in your e-mails as you'd like the prospects to see them, set the time intervals in between the individual messages, and the system is ready to go. All you need to do is add names and e-mail addresses as you get them. You can even personalize the messages to have the system add the prospects' names to the greeting line! The messages appear to be coming from you personally, and it's all happening automatically while you're busy doing other things. This is leverage.

You can set up multiple series in an autoresponder account. We talk about autoresponders again when the subject of e-mail newsletters comes up; for now, you want only to have a message go out maybe once a month in order to just say hi.

## VIDEO E-MAIL FOR HIGH RESPONSE RATES

One of the most exciting things you can use is video e-mail. Video e-mail services are low-cost, much like the autoresponder services, and all you need to get started is an account with one of them and a webcam.

The amazing thing about video e-mail is that the response rates are more than 30 times greater than with regular e-mail! Prospects love the personal touch of seeing you talking to them on video. It even creates pseudocelebrity status, much like insurance agents and realtors who include photos of themselves in their advertising.

To use video e-mail, all you do is record your video message; you can do it over as many times as you like until you're happy, then enter the e-mail addresses (it can be one or a long list) and click on Send. It's especially great for personal, individualized video messages. What a great way to send a thank-you note to an important prospect after a meeting!

Regardless of whether you're using high-tech tools such as video e-mail and autoresponders, or you're simply introducing yourself to prospects via regular e-mail, it's certainly the preferred method of communication nowadays and is far superior to the phone.

# 11

## TRADITIONAL DIRECT MAIL THAT WORKS

### CONDENSING YOUR SALES MESSAGE

Applying what we've already covered to direct mail is very straightforward because the concepts you'll need to convey to prospects through a piece of direct mail are the same as those you will want to convey through other means. In fact, the idea of using flyers came to me thanks to success I'd had with direct mail. Flyers were nothing more than a different way to get the piece out to people!

Simply mailing out your flyer exactly the way it is now will get results; all you need to do is make sure the envelope gets opened. Just don't trifold it, tape it shut, and put a stamp on it. Nothing will get labeled "junk mail" faster.

### FORMATS THAT GET RESPONSES

There are three formats for direct mail that work:

1. Use your existing flyer.
2. Create an effective sales letter.
3. Do a postcard campaign. You can't include as much information, but you don't have to worry about getting the envelope opened.

Since using a flyer is self-explanatory, let's go into a sales letter format that will generate calls. The trick is to make sure the page doesn't look busy; it must not appear to be too long. If it looks like it will take too long to read, prospects won't read it.

Your headline can be slightly longer here. Instead of a huge font we want a slightly larger-than-normal bold font with nothing else around it. Real-life examples that the prospect can relate to are great. For example, you can create a headline that reads, "Through the use of our services, XYZ Company realized an overall increase in profitability of 12%!" In other words, you can go for something along the lines of what an executive would expect to find in a letter.

These same flyer versus letter guidelines apply to the body of your letter. To avoid making the page look busy, go with one font size larger than the typical letter. I like 12-point. Most letters are printed in 10-point, and using 12 is just enough to make the difference. Use your flyer content but lengthen it by adding more potential benefits for the prospect. Avoid talking about your company or features that don't address the three main business goals that every prospect needs to achieve.

Bullet points make any letter look easier to read, and because readers' eyes are drawn to bullet points, they're a great way to list the main benefits of your product or service. Most readers will glance at them first before reading the letter, and if the information conveyed in those bullet points isn't compelling, the rest of the letter won't get read and that prospect won't become a lead.

The closing paragraph must include a call to action just like your other materials. Depending on who the prospect is—a big one or an important account—you may want to inform the prospect that you'll be calling them, and especially to name a specific date and time, put it on your calendar, and make sure you call at that exact time!

Be sure to include all of your contact information, including your personal web address.

## GET YOUR LETTERS OPENED

The biggest challenge in direct mail is getting the prospect to open the envelope. Avoid all of the following:

- Don't use company-printed envelopes.
- Don't use a stick-on address label.
- Don't computer-print the address on the envelopes.

- Don't use a postage meter.
- Don't write "important" or "personal and confidential" on the envelope.

Here's how to get your letter opened:

1. Hand-write the address. This is time-consuming but it's the biggest thing you can do to get your letter opened. The exception to this rule is if you can set up your word-processing software to print in a script font that looks like actual handwriting. You must use a top-quality laser printer to accomplish this.
2. Avoid using a return address. The absence of a return address piques a prospect's curiosity and compels them to open the envelope. The worst possible thing you can do is to use a preprinted company envelope.
3. Use a real stamp. Postage meters are another junk mail indicator. If you use a real stamp, you make your piece look like a personal letter.
4. Use a gimmick on the outside of the envelope. I'm not talking about writing "Important" or anything like that. The trick that worked best for me was to use a rubber date stamp on the bottom front of the envelope along with one that said the word "Approved." Prospects admitted to opening it only because they were intrigued by that.

## FOLLOWING UP ON YOUR MAILER

As you've probably guessed, I think the absolute best way to follow up on a mailer is the method described in the phone chapter. If this isn't possible, e-mail is the next best option. If e-mail addresses are not available, it's okay to make the calls yourself. Remember, doing it yourself is better than no follow-up, and that these aren't really cold calls since the prospect has received your mailer and knows what it's about. If they take your call in the first place, you know they're interested.

## EMPLOY LEVERAGE: AUTOMATED, INEXPENSIVE DIRECT MAIL

One of my favorite new tools is the ability to go to a web site, upload your mailing list, upload the content you want on a postcard, and have the entire campaign printed and mailed for you in one day!

Postcards are a good way to conduct a low-cost mailing, and it provides the added benefit of not having an envelope; it won't get tossed without first getting read.

In creating a postcard, use an attention-grabbing headline, two or three bullet-point benefits, and your contact information. That's it; you don't get much room on a postcard and you still have to leave a clean look that will get read.

While you can manually conduct a postcard mailing yourself, using one of the automated services really speeds things up and gives you a great form of leverage simply because it's a preexisting system. Machines are printing and mailing while you're free to do other things. Several of these services are available, including directly through the U.S. Postal Service on their web site. You upload or enter the content to be printed on the postcard, upload your list, pay the fee, and it's done! Your campaign is automatically printed and mailed out the very next business day. The cost is very low and there are no minimums or maximums, so even if you have only a short list, you can do this.

# 12

## THE WORLD WIDE PROSPECTING WEB

### WHY YOU NEED A PERSONAL WEB SITE

Nothing says Information Age more than the Internet. The World Wide Web is barely a decade old, and yet it has become the literal hub of all communications, all over the world. Almost every business has a web site—those that will last, that is—and almost anything can be purchased online. The Web is the best thing to ever happen to purchasers, regardless of whether they're consumers or CEOs. It gives them a quick and easy way to do product and company research and make a buying decision online. For this reason, it also happens to be the best thing to ever happen to salespeople, but only if they take advantage of it and use it!

Chances are your company or firm has a web site, but do you have your own web site? One that features you and the benefits you can provide for others? If not, you need to get one right away. If you have a well-organized, informative web site, it will act like a net that you have cast that will catch leads for you, automatically, while you're doing other things. The Internet is the most powerful form of leverage now available. However, very few salespeople are using this to their advantage and are missing out on a lot of qualified leads. Those leads are going to salespeople who have set themselves up with a good lead-generation web site.

## USE YOUR WEB ADDRESS EVERYWHERE

Once you have your own site generating leads for you, why not put the web address everywhere? Why let prospects go to a generic company web site when you can have them go directly to yours, one that will speak directly to their needs and the benefits you can provide to them?

For this reason, it's extremely important to include your personal web address on all correspondence and marketing materials. It's especially important on something brief such as a postcard. In fact, the main purpose of postcards and other brief marketing pieces is to drive people to your site.

## BUILDING A SITE QUICKLY AND INEXPENSIVELY

Some of the common myths about web sites are that they're expensive or require the services of a web designer. Nothing could be further from the truth. Many tools are now available that give anyone the ability to create a professional site quickly and easily and at miniscule cost. Web designers are becoming obsolete except for very complicated sites. Here are the best options available to you:

- Use simple web publishing software such as Microsoft FrontPage or Adobe GoLive. This is especially attractive because there are literally thousands of excellent site templates available at little or no cost for these programs. All you do is download the template, cut-and-paste your text and graphics into it, and upload the site to your web address.
- Use an online publishing service such as Yahoo! SiteBuilder or GoDaddy.com. These services let you choose a web template online, cut-and-paste your text and graphics into it, and get the site online instantly. These services are cheaper—as low as $5 per month, all-inclusive—although they don't offer as much customization.
- If you decide to use the second option, choose a domain registrar first (a company that sells domain names). There are too many hassles involved in transferring a domain name from a registrar to a hosting company, and the transition never goes smoothly. It's much easier to buy your domain name from the same company where you plan to host your site. The companies I've already men-

tioned, Yahoo! and GoDaddy.com are just two examples of many that can offer you everything you'll need.

When choosing a domain name, keep it as short and simple as possible. You don't want something long because prospects won't bother typing it in. It's also not that important that the name is entirely relevant to what you're selling. It's the content that matters, not the name. In many cases, striving to come up with a totally relevant name makes it too long and you'll lose traffic as a result. Furthermore, some of the methods of driving traffic we discuss later make the name irrelevant because the user will click on what they see in search engine results, not on a web address. Finally, a short and simple name is easier to remember, which helps in driving return visitors back to your site.

Once you get your domain name registered and have chosen a web creation option, you need to sit down and write out an outline of what content you want on your site. At a minimum, I recommend the following pages:

1. Home page. Here you will include the usual information you'd have on a flyer: headline, brief body text—perhaps with a few bullet points, closing and call to action—and your contact information.

2. About us. Here you'll include information about both you and your company. A photograph of yourself is a nice touch and prospects always seem delighted to recognize you when you come in for an appointment. Although I normally recommend against including a company story, it's okay here because the prospect has the option to view or not view this page. (In fact, statistics show that the About Us page on most web sites is the least viewed.)

3. Product/Service/Benefits. Here you want to list what you're selling and the benefits your products can provide. Remember to keep the three main business goals in mind and make sure you address them directly or your site will not be effective. In fact, a failure to be specific here will not only drive away the good prospects but will attract calls from lousy prospects who don't really know what they want.

4. Testimonials. These are very effective if you have them. If you don't, contact your most satisfied customers and ask for them.

You'll usually write them yourself and simply have customers approve them. Prospects prefer this because its easier for them. Keep testimonials brief; one or two short paragraphs will suffice. If you're new and have no customers you can work with, check with your sales manager. Many offices maintain a standard list of testimonials for use in proposals.

5. Contact page. This is the most important page of all; you want prospects to contact you! Include your telephone number, e-mail address, and possibly a contact form. Contact forms look a bit more professional than simply listing an e-mail address and they're included with most web templates such as the kind you'll be using.

6. As to getting back to people who contact you, I maintain a powerful image by not being in a hurry. I've always preferred to call people back who contacted me in the morning in the mid- to-late afternoon, and to call people who contacted me in the afternoon the following morning. That way you look busy, which is key because having a personal sales web site is really going to enhance your image compared with all of your competition, and prospects will expect you to be a busy person.

The most important thing to remember when putting together a web site is to keep it simple. You want to convey just enough information to get prospects to call you, and just as with your flyers, you want to have a very clean look with plenty of open area on the pages. The single biggest mistake that professional web designers make is to design web sites that are overcomplicated and drive people away instead of drawing them in.

## DRIVING TRAFFIC TO YOUR SITE

There are three primary ways to drive traffic to your web site. They are:

1. Include your web address on all marketing and correspondence.
2. Paid search engine listings.
3. Traditional search engine listings.

The first is self-explanatory. The second option, pay-per-click marketing, is one of the most exciting advances to hit the Internet recently. Pay-per-click, or PPC for short, is simply a way to make your site highly visible in search engine results, and you pay only when someone clicks through to your site (known as a "clickthrough"). In other words, it's free unless and until someone visits your site! You can even set up PPC to target geographically. If you're selling something within a confined area, you can set it up so your listing is seen only by people in your area. This is customizable and you can choose as many or as few regions, states, and countries as you want. That way, if you have a multistate territory, for example, you can show only your listing in states where you're authorized to sell.

The leading PPC services are Google AdWords and Yahoo! Search Marketing. While all are good, Google AdWords provides the widest reach and lowest up-front cost since they bill in arrears; you pay only after you accumulate clickthrough charges.

Setting up a PPC campaign is simply a matter of choosing your campaign settings, which will primarily have to do with geographic targeting, typing in your ad copy as it will appear in search results, and entering a list of keywords and search phrases. These are the searches under which you want your listing to show up. You should strive to make them extremely relevant while leaving out very broad terms. For example, if you sell computer repair services, "computers" would be far too broad a search term for you. You also have the ability to exclude specific keywords from triggering your ad. For example, I almost always include the word "free" as a negative keyword. This is important because you are charged every time someone clicks to your site. Think of every possible type of prospect you don't want and include negative keywords to keep them out. Another example might be a mortgage broker who works only with prime credit and includes "bad credit" as a negative keyword.

Once you enter your keywords and ad, you'll be asked to enter a maximum bid amount. This is the most you're willing to pay for someone to click on your site. Start small here and raise the bid if you're not getting traffic. The daily budget in your campaign settings is very important as well. If you set it too low, your listing will show very little. It's okay to set the daily budget high, because even high-traffic sites never hit their daily budgets.

Google AdWords will start showing your listings immediately. The other services require editorial approval of your ad copy and keywords and take about a week to get rolling.

Once you're online, and you start getting results from your PPC campaign, you may want to seek expert assistance. PPC management services are worth considering because they know all the secrets as to how to increase both the quality and quantity of traffic to your site while minimizing costs.

Finally, don't be intimidated by the fear of high cost in PPC marketing. Many salespeople who are getting great results are spending less than $100 per month. I know someone who places high-dollar commercial loans; he spent less than $25 in one month and made six figures in commissions as a result of the leads generated.

I recommend against pursuing regular, otherwise known as "natural" or "organic," search engine listings. It's simply too difficult to accomplish and most search engine optimization firms can't accomplish anything either, make no guarantees, and charge exorbitant fees. Don't waste your money on them.

## THE WEB IS THE ULTIMATE FORM OF LEVERAGE

Never underestimate the power of the World Wide Web. Of all the forms of self-marketing available to you, the Web is the most powerful if you use it correctly. Consider some of the things that have happened over the past decade all because of the Internet: Old, established corporations have gone bankrupt for failing to keep up with the times and leverage themselves on the Internet, and young people with no formal education have become multimillionaires. The Internet is one form of leverage that can make you if you use it and can break you if you don't. It can break you simply because your competitors will use it to get business you're missing out on. Most salespeople will eventually realize this and get their own sites someday. Do it now, and the bulk of the business will be yours.

# 13

## KEEPING IN TOUCH, AUTOMATICALLY

### THE IMPORTANCE OF ONGOING CONTACT

One of the biggest things I had trouble doing as a salesperson was keeping in contact with people who didn't buy from me. As you spend more time in sales and make more contacts, it becomes extremely difficult to make regular and ongoing contact with them. I was never able to get organized enough to do this. Even with advances in customer relationship management (CRM) and lead-management software, it's still difficult, and even if you do manage to keep tabs on everyone, there comes a time when you've accumulated so many potential contacts that there isn't enough time to maintain contact with them all. I know salespeople who have dozens of shoeboxes full of business cards. There's no way to maintain personal direct contact with that many people!

Ongoing contact is important simply because most of the people we come into contact with either aren't going to buy from us, or they already have their needs taken care of elsewhere. So, what do most salespeople do? They file a card away and never make an effort to contact that person again in the future. Salespeople could triple their production by maintaining an open line of communication with each and every prospect who has no current need, because all prospects eventually have needs in the future. It goes back to the fact that cold calling makes timing work against you. The trick is to beat the system by neutralizing time and virtually be in front of the prospect always. Remember, a salesperson who expects to succeed in our new economy must effectively be in all places at all times.

## ADVANTAGES OF A FREE NEWSLETTER

A free newsletter is the highly effective solution I came up with to beat timing and start multiplying my sales production with prospects whom I otherwise would have forgotten, and who would have forgotten about me. A free newsletter does the following:

- It provides prospects with free, valuable information. My own experience has proved that you must give before you can expect to receive. By maintaining a free newsletter, you provide prospects with useful information that can benefit them right now.
- It keeps prospects in your marketing system. Instead of simply dropping a lead who isn't going to buy now, a free newsletter keeps those prospects in your system indefinitely.
- It keeps your name in the prospects' minds. There is no way a busy prospect will remember your name when they have never purchased anything from you. A free newsletter constantly reminds them that you're out there and that you can help them achieve their goals.
- It separates you from your competition. Few salespeople do anything for prospects unless it will result in an immediate sale. I used to be guilty of this myself. We all want instant gratification and don't want to spend time with prospects who will buy in the distant future. By sending out a free newsletter, you're not spending any time at all on prospects who aren't ready to buy now, but to the prospects it seems that you are.

## HOW A FREE NEWSLETTER BUILDS
## MOMENTUM THROUGH LEVERAGE

In addition to the advantages we just looked at, newsletter results are cumulative. As your list continues to build, your list of potential prospects continues to build as well.

Let's say, for example, that you're currently making 40 cold calls per day for a total of 800 a month in order to trickle down to 10 sales. That means you're making 800 new contacts every month, few of which you'll ever talk to again simply because they have no current needs. Now let's say you've started a free newsletter and you begin asking those 800 contacts for permission to send it to them. Few prospects say no, but we'll be conservative and say that only half give you permission. That means you're adding 400 new contacts to your list each month. After a year that's 4,800 potential buyers in just this one system alone! That means instead of contacting only 800 potential prospects every month, you're contacting several thousands, automatically! If a very conservative 1 percent contact you each month, that's 48 red hot new leads that will be very easy to close. No wonder I tripled my income by using a free newsletter!

## IF IT DOESN'T HELP THEM, THEY WON'T READ IT

The key to making this effective is to avoid sending out a blatant sales pitch. Sure, you want these people to buy something, but sending out ads isn't going to accomplish anything. They get plenty of ads already. What you want to do is offer up free information that they can genuinely use and is related to what you're selling. Here are some examples:

- Realtors can offer tips for first-time buyers, property value and tax information, home remodeling and renovation tips, and so on.
- Financial advisors can provide information on maximizing income from investments, what kind and how much insurance people in different situations really need, and so on.
- Dentists can offer free tips and information to better enable prospective patients to take care of their teeth.

When I sold telecom services, I offered up free information on how prospects could protect their networks from hackers, defend against viruses, tips on increasing e-commerce revenue, and other useful information related to my industry. This was information that consultants would normally charge for.

## BUILDING YOUR NEWSLETTER LIST

The simplest way to build your list is to begin adding every contact you have, and to ask every new contact you make if they'd like to receive your newsletter.

Another great way is to mention on all of your marketing materials that you have a free newsletter available. You could even add this to your business cards. All you need is something such as, "Ask to sign up for my free newsletter!" If you're using a commercial e-mail service to maintain an e-mail newsletter, you can add a sign-up form to your web site. Otherwise, simply include an e-mail address or contact form on your site that people can use to request your newsletter. I especially like using this on fax-back forms on flyers or mailers. Include a line that says, "I'm not interested but would like to receive your free newsletter. My e-mail address is _____."

As for delivering your newsletter, the three ways are mail, fax, and e-mail. I prefer e-mail because it will get read a lot more frequently than a regular piece of mail or a fax. Regular mail will be seen as junk mail and a fax newsletter can easily be mistaken for a junk fax and discarded.

The two options for running an e-mail newsletter are to do it manually or to use an e-mail newsletter service. I highly recommend the latter. They're very inexpensive, are easy to use, and deliver a professional appearance. They're easy to manage and even include a remove link so people can unsubscribe. If you do this manually you'll have to spend time taking people off your list. A quick online search will reveal dozens of services that provide a great value. Most of them even give you sign-up forms that you can add to your web site just like the ones I use on my sites.

## EVEN MORE LEVERAGE THROUGH AUTORESPONDERS

I've already touched on autoresponders but want to bring them up again here because they are an especially important application. Again, an autoresponder is nothing more than a preprogrammed list of e-mails that is set to go out to your list at predetermined intervals. So, for example, you can type out a dozen newsletters and program the autoresponder system to send them to your list a month apart. That way, you've taken care of an entire years' worth of e-mail newsletters right up front! What's more, as people are added to your list, they all start at the beginning and won't miss any of your newsletters.

You can also broadcast live e-mails in addition to the autoresponder series. That way, your prospects get the regular newsletters once a month and also receive current information. This is the best of both worlds; nobody misses out on your regular newsletters, and you can still keep them up-to-date on the latest information.

As you can see, just this one system alone would give a major boost to any salesperson's results. Combine it with other systems and you'll be unstoppable!

# 14

## WEBLOGS

### WHAT IS A "BLOG"?

A "blog" is simply a public diary online. It's also a wonderful marketing tool. It works like a newsletter; it provides free, useful information to people while generating hot leads. I maintain a blog (nevercoldcall.typepad.com), and it not only provides free information and a form of entertainment to people, but also drives tons of business.

### HOW A BLOG ATTRACTS QUALIFIED PROSPECTS

Blogs are effective at attracting qualified prospects because they're not selling anything. They're simply outlets for the author's thoughts. While most sites are meant to sell something, a blog merely sets out to inform and entertain. People are less resistant to a noncommercial site like a blog and are more likely to read it.

The clincher is that there's always an "About Me" page, as well as a link to the site that does sell something. On my blog, my About Me page immediately informs the reader that I'm an author in the field of sales and provides the link to my regular product sites. Everyone who enjoys reading my blog inevitably clicks through to my other sites.

### SETTING UP YOUR BLOG

Setting up a blog is very easy because, unlike a Web site, there's nothing to design or lay out unless you specifically want to. There are even several free blog services. It's a simple matter of registering, choosing a layout, entering a title and your About Me page, and you're all set. It's one of the simplest things you can do online.

## DRIVING TRAFFIC TO YOUR BLOG

Since your blog will have its own unique web address, you can include that wherever you include your regular web address. As blogs gain in popularity, more and more people are becoming aware of what they are, so saying "Visit my blog" isn't a big deal, and those who don't know what a blog is will be even more curious to visit it.

You can include a link to your blog along with the "Visit my blog" line on your web site. This is probably best left to your About Us and Contact Me pages. It's great for your short personal bio on the About Us page, and it's a natural to include with your contact information.

Because a blog is a natural choice for attempting to sway prospects who may not have responded to other marketing efforts, I don't reveal my blog address upfront, but rather include it in my autoresponder series, about six e-mails, in a brief "Visit my blog" message. Prospects click through to it and many come back to the main site and buy as a result.

Finally, blogs tend to rank higher in regular search engine results than do commercial web sites. This is because they're "keyword rich," meaning blogs tend to be one long page with lots of text and numerous entries, rather than a web site that is split into several pages with only a moderate amount of text on each one. When you set up your blog, one of the parameters you can control is how many entries will appear on the page. Set this number high so the blog will rank high in search results and will receive a lot more traffic.

## THE GOAL OF DRIVING TRAFFIC TO YOUR BLOG

Remember, all you want to do is provide enough good information to get a prospect really interested and to either sign up for your newsletter, visit your main sales site, or, best of all, call you immediately.

# 15

## GAIN PROSPECTS' TRUST THROUGH FREE SEMINARS

### BECOME THE AUTHORIZED EXPERT

After I had spent a few years in sales and had begun learning how to sell without cold calling, I tried something new. I created a flyer that sold nothing but invited people to come attend a free luncheon where they could learn how to use the Internet to improve their businesses. We noted on the flyers that the luncheon would be limited to 20 attendees and included an RSVP fax-back form.

I distributed those flyers door-to-door like I'd always done up to that point, but confined them to an area within a few miles of the restaurant I'd reserved for our event. Instead of just dropping the flyers off, I spent 20 seconds telling each person what it was about and that it was absolutely free. I got a dozen replies.

I'd reserved a room in a local restaurant near a major business park. I arrived early to make sure the table and chairs were set up and that the attendees would get only the lunch specials menu, all of which cost no more than $5. As each person arrived, I greeted them, exchanged business cards, and had them sit at the large table and order lunch. Once everyone had arrived, about 10 minutes after the announced time, I went into my talk on how businesses could profit through effective use of the Internet. My presentation included a white board and flip chart in order to communicate most effectively.

The attendees really appreciated the information because I kept it impartial and avoided selling. They enjoyed the free food, too! After the hour came to a close, several of the attendees asked me to call. In short, the end result of spending one hour and less than $100 in lunches quickly resulted in a few sales and several hundred dollars in commissions.

The keys to success in doing this were as follows:

- There was no overt sales pitch. The invitations made it clear that this was an information-only event. I even kept my company name off the flyers, and simply listed myself as a consultant.
- I offered an incentive to attend. The free lunch was key. It would be far more difficult to get people to give up an hour otherwise. In addition, scheduling conflicts are less likely during the lunch hour.
- It was convenient. I deliberately chose a restaurant adjacent to a business park and distributed invitations only in the immediate area.
- I gave them what I had promised. Every attendee got their free lunch and information that would be of value whether they bought anything or not.

### KEEP IT SIMPLE AND MANAGEABLE

In setting up a free seminar, you must keep it to a size that is manageable and affordable for you. As time goes on and you make more money as a result of these methods, you can expand the size and scope of your events. For example, I coached someone who started with small luncheon seminars. He has since grown his business to the point where he rents out large halls and conducts evening seminars for hundreds of people, complete with a catered buffet. For invitations he mails out thousands of postcards announcing the event. You can accomplish the same thing as a result of your campaign and eventually have hundreds of people coming to hear what you have to say. For now, start small; find restaurants near concentrations of potential prospects that have private rooms you can reserve for free and affordable lunch menus, and present to groups of a dozen or so people.

## GETTING PEOPLE TO ATTEND

There are any number of ways to announce your free seminar, but invitations are most effective when you can target them to a geographic area that is very close to the site of your event. Few people will drive across town to attend unless they're extremely interested in the topic of choice, but even those with only a mild interest or curiosity will go somewhere that's only a few minutes away.

I like flyers best for announcing luncheon seminars. Mail is also an option although you'll need a list that's either within that area or that can be broken down as such. Going by ZIP codes and mailing only to the ZIP code where your event will take place is ideal. E-mail is good in that is costs nothing, but the flip side is that it's practically impossible to divide e-mail addresses geographically. You can always send out an announcement to your entire list, but chances are only those who are nearby will attend.

If you get a poor response to your invitations, you may have made it sound like a sales pitch. You may have also failed to put enough emphasis on the incentive. Don't just say, "Lunch will be provided at no cost." Say something like, "You'll enjoy the sumptuous creations of ABC Restaurant, compliments of us!" Avoid any sales lingo. Use a neutral title for yourself, such as consultant. Never use "account executive" or anything similar.

The next question is how many flyers to distribute. More is better, and too many is better than not enough. Don't expect a tremendous response; distribute as many as possible. If you don't get enough responses, you'll wind up having to cancel the event. On the other hand, if you get too many, you can accept as many RSVPs as you can accommodate and inform the rest that the event is already sold out but another will be coming up soon. This does two things: First, it gives you a list of people you already know will want to attend the next one, and second, it raises your value because everyone wants what is in demand.

The final aspect is timing. I recommend 10 days to 2 weeks before. Any sooner and the chances are too high that people will already have prior commitments. Any longer and people will forget or lose interest and fail to show up.

## CONDUCTING YOUR FREE SEMINAR

The day before, call every attendee to confirm that they'll be in attendance. If anyone cancels, and you were lucky enough to get a good response and sell out, you can call one of your "alternates." You can also e-mail a reminder a few days before. Since most of your RSVPs will probably come from your fax-back form, and you should always ask for an e-mail address on those, you should have most of them already. If anyone RSVPs via telephone, ask for an e-mail address for the purpose of sending out a reminder a few days before. And, of course, your free newsletter! Never overlook an opportunity to expand your newsletter list. It will be worth gold to you over time. You should also call the restaurant where you plan to hold your seminar a few days in advance to confirm your reservation. If for some reason they've messed up, you'll have enough time to find an alternative venue and inform your attendees of the new location.

On the day of your free seminar, get your materials in order that morning. This may include flip charts, a white board, or a projector. Always have a good handout that follows your presentation. I recommend arriving at your venue at least 20 minutes early, and possibly even a little earlier if you have to set up a projector. Get your room in order and set the tables and chairs up as you'd like them. I prefer a long table with the presentation materials set up at one end where I'll be standing. This allows the attendees to comfortably eat their lunches while being able to watch and listen to what you're doing. Be sure the place settings are set, and place handouts on the table at each seat.

As your guests arrive, warmly greet each of them and exchange business cards. I recommend getting cards now, before your luncheon begins, because it will be harder to get them as people are leaving or if someone has to leave early. Take a few moments to chat with each guest. While I don't recommend personal rapport building in a regular sales appointment, I think it's very important here; after all, this is an informational session and not a sales pitch, and you want to create a warm, comfortable setting. Remember everyone's name. Silently repeat each name to yourself several times if you have to upon meeting each person.

Allow everyone to order lunch before beginning your presentation. It's a good idea to sit at the table and make small talk with everyone until that's done. Once everyone has ordered, stand up and get started. Keep an open forum and present in a conversational style, encouraging participation and questions. Stick to your presentation outline, and be sure to follow the order that's laid out in the participants' handouts. I generally recommend wrapping up the formal presentation piece about 15 minutes before ending time in order to answer questions and encourage conversation both between yourself and the participants, and among themselves.

Once you've finished, be sure to sincerely thank each person for coming as they leave. Several will ask you to contact them, which is why it's important to remember names right from the start! You don't want to be in your office the next day with a stack of cards and no clue as to who is who. You'll probably also be contacted by some of the attendees requesting more information. Whatever you do, don't try to sell or set appointments while people are leaving; all you want to do is to let them know they can call or e-mail you anytime if they have questions or an interest in buying.

## CONVERT ATTENDEES TO CUSTOMERS

Now that your seminar is complete, it's time to turn your attendees into customers. Mail or e-mail a thank-you note to everyone who came. This is a nice gesture, especially since you gave them something for free and there's no expectation for you to thank them for coming.

As I've already mentioned, you'll get some calls and e-mails over the next few days from people who would like to speak further. Check them off your list and keep a separate list of those who haven't contacted you. Wait a week, then call each of them to set up an appointment. This is one of the few exceptions to my usual rules on calling; since they've met you, you should call personally. Some will accept an appointment and some won't. For those who aren't interested or who have no current need, get their okay to add them to your newsletter list. When the time comes that they do have a need, you'll be certain to get the sale.

As time goes on and you generate more income, you'll be able to expand the size and scope of your seminars. If you sell to consumers, evening and weekend seminars will be an option for you. In the end, free seminars will not only generate sales that would have never come to you otherwise, but will build a reputation for yourself as a knowledgeable and generous person, and that will do only good things for your career.

# 16

## EASILY OBTAIN FREE PUBLICITY

### REPORTERS COLD CALL, TOO!

A few years ago I ran a small telecom sales agency representing most of the service providers in my area. Although I had agents selling for me, I still sold a bit myself and also worked with the companies we represented on ways to market our services.

One of the Internet companies in particular was growing at the time, and we decided to contact the reporter with our local business journal who covered technology. After a phone call and lunch, we got our first article printed. We talked about the unique things the company was doing to benefit customers and included the company's web address. For weeks after that first article ran, the calls and inquiries came pouring in. We generated a lot of business for the mere cost of that one lunch.

A few months later, this same reporter needed another story, so we thought of some new things to talk about, and another story ran. Once again, the phones rang and leads came pouring in, which resulted in several more easy sales.

Another few months down the road, the reporter needed another fresh story, and we, of course, were more than willing to help. Yet again, dozens of hot leads came in, ready and willing to buy from us, and we didn't have to lift a finger to get them. The best part was that they were so excited about our services that they just bought—no selling required!

That was the end of our run with the business journal, but there's another twist to this story. One of the accounts I had personally sold was in the process of releasing exciting new software. Even though I had nothing to do with their achievement, I did sell them Internet access, and that was a necessity for them. I got in touch with the reporter who handled technology stories for one of the local papers and had him visit that company. The owners told him all about their exciting product, I briefly explained that I was responsible for bringing them broadband Internet access, and we all posed together for a nice color photo that appeared on the front page of the business section along with our story! One paragraph mentioned my name and the name of my company, along with the fact that they were dependent on my services in order to stay in business.

Once again, the calls came in. The irony here is that I was really no different from hundreds of other local Internet salespeople, but just being associated with something like that and getting my picture in the paper was a differentiating factor for prospects, and I was favored over the competition. It's a fairly safe bet to say the people who called in and bought from me thanks to that article were many of the same people who wouldn't take cold calls from representatives offering exactly what they needed. Again, I got all of this business with zero effort other than the few hours spent arranging that meeting with the reporter.

This is so easy to accomplish because reporters cold call, too, and they don't like it any more than we do! Few people realize this because they think media coverage is difficult to get, but in reality reporters must constantly find new stories, and that's not easy. There just aren't that many interesting things happening so they have to go out and find something to write about. When you do them the favor of calling to let them know that you have a great story, they will be more than happy. In fact, they'll keep coming back to you for more stories in the future, just like our business journal reporter did.

I currently write articles for dozens of publications free of charge. When people ask why I don't request compensation, I state my belief that you gain the most when you first give with no expectation of reward. My free articles help thousands of people, and my reward for that is increased business. The same holds true for working with reporters. If you are willing to spend your time giving a reporter something interesting to write about and buy lunch in the process, you'll make that reporter very happy, you'll provide information to readers, and your reward will be increased business and lots of new customers whom you would have never found otherwise. This is one of the best ways to attract high-value prospects who do not take cold calls.

## WHY THE MEDIA NEEDS YOU

As we all know, all forms of media make money through advertising. Advertising rates are determined by circulation. The more readers, the higher the prices. This is why classified ads in local newspapers are cheap while ads in major magazines cost tens of thousands of dollars. A commercial during an event like the Super Bowl costs millions of dollars. The more viewers, the higher the price.

In order to increase circulation, publications need to attract more readers, and this is done through the quality of the articles. The big magazines get tens of thousands of dollars for one ad because hundreds of thousands of people will see it. The Super Bowl gets millions of dollars for an ad because tens of millions of people will see it. A classified ad is cheap because only a few hundred people will see it. Print publications need your story because more good stories equal higher circulation and higher ad rates.

## MAKING THE INITIAL CONTACT

Find out whom you need to contact. I recommend starting out with a local business journal or a small local newspaper. Find an article that's related to your industry, or that is in the business column, and write down the reporter's name and contact information. Nearly all publications include an e-mail address or phone number; if not, call the publication's main number to ask for that person.

Before calling or e-mailing, you need to know why you're newsworthy. Nobody is going to publish an article that's an obvious sales pitch. You must either talk about something worthy of interest or you must provide useful information that readers will appreciate. When I write an article, I provide helpful tips and suggestions for salespeople. An example of mine was for sales managers and explained how to positively motivate someone who is not performing. Think about what you can say that will help people. Someone I know who sells financial services contributes articles explaining how people can minimize tax liability. If you're doing something interesting, talk about it. The Internet company I mentioned earlier specialized in extremely fast installation, sometimes same-day. This was newsworthy and people were thrilled to find out about it.

Once you've decided what your particular angle will be, call or send an e-mail to your chosen reporter. Introduce yourself, briefly describe what you do along with why your story is one that would be great to run, and invite the person to lunch.

When you meet, be prepared to tell your story, sticking with the theme of announcing something newsworthy or contributing useful information that would be beneficial to readers. Bring along any documentation that will be helpful in telling your story; just avoid the typical company story material since no one is interested in that, especially reporters.

Chances are this will be all it takes to get your first article run. However, don't pursue publicity until you have your web site online. Including your web address in the article is critical. Phone numbers typically aren't included, and if they mention only the company name or the company web address, others will get the leads and profit by your efforts. By sticking with your personal web address, you'll be the one to get the leads you've worked to generate, and prospects will be happy to contact the person they read about in the article instead of reaching a random salesperson.

## USE LEVERAGE TO GET MORE PUBLICITY

Once your first article has run, it's easier to get more. Since reporters are constantly on the lookout for something to write about, they read competing publications to see what's been published. It's common to get calls from reporters at other publications after your first article. The more you get published, the more this will happen. I've had students who had their first business journal article run, and immediately received offers for more and even invitations onto local radio shows and morning television shows. We've all seen local businesspeople featured on local morning news shows. Now you know how they got there and how you can, too!

It's a great idea to order article reprints from publications and use them to create a media kit. If reprints aren't available, obtain permission to duplicate the article for use in your media kit. This is simply a packet of information you'll send to other reporters. It should include article reprints, a cover letter explaining what you do and why you're newsworthy, and a business card. Since you've included an article that's already run, you have legitimacy, and other reporters will be eager to write about you.

Once you've gotten media exposure, you'll be regarded as an expert in your field. This newfound status will give you so much power that competition becomes a nonissue and you'll have an endless supply of leads. Publicity is free advertising, but it's also seen as fact. The results are truly staggering!

# 17

## BE A REAL CONSULTATIVE SALESPERSON

### BE A TRUE CONSULTANT, NOT ANOTHER SALES REP

"Consultative selling" is one of the most sensible selling methods in theory. It simply means that you make a recommendation based upon prospects' true needs rather than just selling them what you want to sell. This serves them better and the resulting sale is a true win-win situation.

The reality is that there is a limit on how consultative a salesperson can really be. After all, you can recommend only your own products while a legitimate consultant can recommend anything. They're not selling anything other than their professional advice.

Because of this, and the fact that the term "consultative selling" has become so overused, prospects have come to resent it. They're getting tired of having salespeople come in and tell them that the seller will make recommendations based strictly upon their needs, when they know very well that salespeople can recommend only their own products. No salesperson would ever recommend a competitor, and therefore none are truly consultative.

In addition. legitimate consultants get furious at salespeople claiming to be consultants. They are experts in their respective fields and make recommendations that really benefit their clients. They're insulted by salespeople who promise to do the same.

However, there is a way to rise above all this and not only profit but really help people in the process. It's to actually become a consultant. I'm not talking about switching careers; I mean offering your unbiased opinions and advice to prospects even if they have no intention of buying from you anytime soon.

This isn't difficult, and it won't overwhelm you like you may think it would. It goes back to the fact that salespeople desire money—we're in sales because of the income potential—and the reality that salespeople are usually loath to spend time with someone who isn't going to buy right away. I used to be like that and never wanted to meet prospects who needed information for a purchase that was months out and had no immediate need to purchase. Keep in mind that I was in the phone business and we were paid upon installation. That means when I closed a big sale, if it was for a phone system for a new building that wouldn't be completed for another six months, I had to wait that long to get paid. It wasn't very exciting. Later on, I realized how much this attitude was costing me when I began offering my help to people. I only did it at first because I had matured a bit personally and started getting real satisfaction out of helping people, but then I actually started making money as a result.

## COMPENSATION

The principle at work here is explained in great detail in Ralph Waldo Emerson's essay on compensation. I recommend this essay to all salespeople. Read it several times; each time you'll learn new truths that you hadn't picked up during previous readings. The essay is in the public domain and can be readily found online.

Although the essay goes into deep detail, the point is that you have to give before you can expect to receive. The longer it takes for your compensation to come, the more you receive. I know this to be true as a result of offering my time to people who had no immediate needs. Interesting things happened as a result of my help:

- When those people did have a need, they called me and only me, and there was no competition involved in the sale. In addition, price was a nonissue.

- When these people had a need for a product I didn't offer, they always called me for recommendations. This resulted in lots of money earned from referral fees and commission splits and made me a desired networking partner. It brought me several lucrative contacts.
- This is the biggest one: These people offered my name and card to everyone. They talked me up so much that the referrals I received were ready to buy. Again, there was no competition and few price objections.

### APPLYING THE LAW OF COMPENSATION

An example of how I applied the law was by keeping telephone technician tools in my car. If I came across someone who just needed a line added or a jack moved, I spent 10 minutes doing it for them. They were not only grateful that a salesman in a suit would roll up his sleeves and take the time to do this, but also for the money they'd saved by not having to pay for an hours' worth of technician time plus a visit charge. You can imagine how much respect and trust I earned from these people and why there was never even a question about buying from me.

Regardless of what business you're in, you can easily find ways to do this. An attorney won me as a client when I called around for a consultation on an issue I was dealing with at the time. Instead of a paid consultation, he answered my questions at no charge. I greatly appreciated this. Since then I've referred several people to him. Think about ways and means you can apply this principle to yourself and you will profit beyond your wildest dreams.

# 18

## REAL NETWORKING THAT REALLY WORKS

### THE HOLY GRAIL OF SALES THAT'S SO HARD TO FIND

Two things that are traditionally taught to salespeople concerning lead generation are cold calling and networking. While I obviously disagree with cold calling, I fully endorse networking. The problem is that finding or building a good network is easier said than done.

I wasted more time than you can imagine looking for a good networking group. My managers encouraged it, and some even required that I get involved with networking groups, including chambers of commerce. I agreed with their thinking, but what I found was terribly disappointing.

It all started when one of my managers gave me a complimentary invitation to a morning leads club. I'd be able to attend one breakfast meeting and then decide if I'd like to join. Although I was looking forward to going, I'm not a morning person, to the point where getting up too early ruins my entire day. I arrived at the meeting at seven in the morning. Every other salesperson there appeared to be just as bleary-eyed and miserable to be up so early as I was, except for the moderator.

Everyone ordered breakfast and the meeting commenced. Everyone said, "I don't have any leads this week." Then someone got up and spoke for a few minutes pitching a new cleaning business. There was some conversation amongst the participants, the meeting ended, and everyone left.

Before I could leave, however, the moderator pressured me to join for a membership fee of several hundred dollars. I thought this was outrageous for something that seemed so unproductive, so I declined. I then received several phone calls before the moderator realized that I wasn't going to join. After all, even if it were free I wouldn't return! It finally dawned on me that this was nothing more than a scam to make as much as possible in membership fees.

Next, I made a sale to customers who had been in the same dilemma and had managed to form their own group. Like me, they considered the idea of an early morning meeting ridiculous, so they started a happy hour leads club that met once a month. It sounded like they'd gotten some good people involved so I was looking forward to the first meeting. I arrived, met everyone else who was there and exchanged some cards, ordered drinks and appetizers, and the meeting commenced. Just like the last one, nobody had any leads. Someone got up for 10 minutes to talk about what they did—taking turns giving their pitch each month—and once that was complete, the rest of the evening consisted of drinking and shooting pool. No networking. I attended a few more meetings but only because it was fun. It was useless as far as networking goes.

I got involved with the chamber of commerce later on when I started working for a company that was a member. By this time, I was skeptical of any type of networking group but gave it a chance anyway. This was even worse because most of the members were out to sell their products to everyone else in attendance. The few chamber mixers I attended were always followed by a barrage of phone calls from people who were all trying to sell me something. Some were especially obnoxious with their endless phone calls and I swore off the chamber for good.

After swearing off networking groups forever, I came across one that really intrigued me. It was a private group, which required me to obtain an invitation from a member to attend one meeting as a guest. At this meeting I'd be introduced to the rest of the membership, and if they felt that I had something to contribute, I would then be interviewed by the two principals of the organization, and would then have to obtain the endorsement of two members in order to be granted membership. I was excited. I knew it must be good if member screening was so thorough.

I put on my best suit and drove to my first meeting where I hoped to make a great impression with the affluent members. I was shocked when I walked in and saw all the same shady characters who had stalked me for weeks after those chamber meetings, trying to sell me their business opportunities. We made our introductions, exchanged cards, and the meeting commenced. A couple of shabbily-dressed web designers did a presentation showcasing some of the sites they'd recently developed. That was it, and everyone went to the bar for drinks. I was deeply offended that I'd been duped into believing that this was a serious, exclusive group.

I don't mean to discourage you with these stories. I'm telling them because most salespeople I've worked with have had similar experiences, and it's important to know that I've been through it all. I didn't let it discourage me, and I always remembered what Thomas Edison said about the fact that he had failed more than 10,000 times in his quest for the electric light bulb. He said, "I kept on going because I knew that after I found all the things that don't work, I was bound to find the thing that did work." He referred to his 10,000 failures as 10,000 successful attempts at finding the things that don't work! That's how I view my early experiences with networking.

## OFFER REAL INCENTIVES

I discovered the answer when I was working for a company that had a referral program in place. Whenever someone gave me a lead that resulted in a sale, that person got paid. Suddenly my networking took off like you would not believe. People who had never given me anything in the past, who had sat at those breakfast meetings with vacant stares saying, "I don't have any leads this week," were suddenly referring hot leads!

The bottom line is that you have to provide people with some real incentive before you can expect them to give you leads. You can never expect someone to do something without providing that person with adequate compensation, and the same holds true for the referral partners you'll be working with. Granted, it shouldn't have to be this way, and everyone should follow the Law of Compensation and freely give, but that just isn't the case in the real world.

There are two things you can offer to others as forms of real, tangible compensation in return for the qualified leads they provide you:

1. Money. If you have a predefined referral plan on paper that you can hand someone, it will motivate them to both think of people they currently know as well as let others know about you.

2. Qualified leads. Remember the chapter on building your success based upon providing free help and assistance to people as a true consultant? I eventually had so many people asking whom I'd recommend for this, that, and the other thing that other salespeople were fighting to network with me. A good network partner is so rare that word of your supply of good referrals will spread like wildfire.

Money is the easier way to get started, especially if you're early in your career or don't yet have a clientele. The two ways to go about this are either a company referral program or out of your own pocket. The company referral program is better. In fact, when I found myself with a company lacking a referral program, I talked to the management about this. They were open to it, especially after I had told them about my previous successes in offering lucrative referral fees to others. They quickly put one together, so if you're with a company that does not have a referral program in place, talk to them because there's a good chance they'll go along with it.

If you don't have a company referral program and they're not willing to start one, consider paying out-of-pocket referral fees. Nobody likes to give up some of their commissions, but remember, that money is from sales you would have never gotten otherwise. Let's say I'm offering 30 percent of my commissions as a referral fee for sales. That means I'm keeping 70 percent of a sale I would have never gotten otherwise. In other words, if I hadn't offered that 30 percent, I'd have nothing. Anyone with sales experience knows that finding a qualified lead is half the work, and once you have one that's truly qualified, you're halfway there. With that in mind, don't be cheap when it comes to referral fees. A percentage of something is better than nothing.

Regardless of whether you're having your company pay out the referral fees or you're doing it yourself, it's imperative to have your plan in writing. This makes it official in the eyes of your networking partners. When meeting with new networking partners, I always provide them with a stack of my cards along with a stack of flyers. Have them initial the flyers before handing them out so you can keep track of their referrals.

## KEEPING YOUR NETWORK UPDATED AND MOTIVATED

One of the big failures of networking is that salespeople recruit networking partners but fail to maintain an ongoing relationship. We meet so many people and it's easy to forget things and remember who's who. Your networking partners are no different, and if you go without contact for a month or longer after recruiting them, they may very well forget about you and fail to recognize opportunities that may have been lucrative for them.

Try to get together for coffee or lunch at least once a month with your networking partners. If you have built a good group, and they're not competing directly with each other, group meetings are fine, and if you have a dozen or more solid people in your network who are producing, I like using the luncheon seminar format to keep them updated with the latest information. Treat this like an agent channel manager handles his agents. The lunch seminar format is exactly how the best ones conduct their business and manage their agents. You should do the same. In fact, if you think of yourself as an agent channel manager and work your program the same way, you'll be most effective.

Get started right away on building a powerful network using these guidelines. At one point in my career I was always well over quota, and all of my sales came from my network. That was the best and easiest period in my sales career. You can experience the same thing, and quickly at that.

# Part Three

---

# You Have
# the Leads—
# Now Get the Sales

# 19

## THE SALES APPOINTMENT PROCESS

### IF THEY'RE QUALIFIED, THIS IS THE EASY PART

When considering the beginning of the sales process starting with the first appointment, people think this is where the real selling begins, but I tend to disagree for two reasons. The first has to do with cold calling. Cold calling is so inefficient and time-consuming that it realistically takes up at least 60 percent of the time associated with a sale. So, if you've uncovered a qualified lead through cold calling, you've already done the tedious work, and the actual selling process is a breeze by comparison. The second reason I disagree is in a self-marketing scenario, where prequalified prospects are calling you. The sales process in this case is usually quick and easy, at least compared with the old way of doing things. It is for these reasons that I hold the opinion that by having a qualified lead in hand, you're already two-thirds of the way to a sale.

### THE KISS TEST

Because most salespeople tend to overcomplicate the sales process and try to drag the prospect through a number of steps that are usually unnecessary, especially when the prospect is definitely qualified and has a current need, I'd like to touch on a principle that I think is very, very important before moving on. It's called The KISS Test, for "Keep It Simple, Stupid."

Here are some examples. I once sat next to someone who was an excellent salesperson except for the fact that he had the nasty habit of always talking himself out of sales. He and I both operated much the same in that rather than cold calling, we ran our own self-marketing programs to generate leads and simply took the calls that came in as a result. The problem is what he did with the calls. When someone called me, ready to buy, I immediately went into closing the deal and making arrangements to either come out with the paperwork or to fax or e-mail it over. This guy, on the other hand, went into a full-length company story, a full-length explanation of the service, and a lot of other information that he absolutely should not tell a clearly qualified prospect unless they specifically asked for it. The end result was that people who called ready to sign up for one of our more expensive services either changed their mind and dropped to the entry-level service, or they lost interest and didn't buy anything at all.

Another example is something that I recently experienced as a prospective buyer. I was searching the Internet for local companies that could provide a particular service I needed. I found the web site of a company that appeared capable of serving my needs, so I called and asked to speak to a salesperson. We spoke for 10 minutes and it was clear that they had exactly what I was looking for, and at the right price. I asked to have contracts e-mailed to me in order that I could sign up and get started right away on setup. Well, getting off the phone wasn't quite that easy. Here I was, already saying, "Yes, I'm going to buy," and this sales rep launches into a full-blown company story about how they've been in business for more than 20 years, how they have so many hundred clients worldwide, and on and on and on. If they hadn't been so appropriate for my needs I might have gotten annoyed and changed my mind, but luckily for this rep, the product sold itself. If that wasn't enough, the e-mail arrived later that day. The requested proposal and contracts were attached, but the e-mail itself was a good two pages of more company story nonsense, more useless drivel about all the big important clients they have, and more waste-of-time bragging about their capabilities. I was half-amazed that my spam filter didn't delete this one upon arrival.

The sad part about all this is that even though I still bought, I'm willing to bet that a lot of people don't. Nothing is more frustrating than picking up the phone saying, "Hi, here I am with a check in hand, ready to buy," and having the salesperson go into a story bragging about how great the company is and all that they can do. To a decision maker who's ready to buy, that comes off as pure arrogance. What's more, talking about all your big enterprise clients alienates most smaller prospects. They assume their needs will be placed second to those of the big dogs and that they'll be treated as just a number when calling for service. Here is a salesperson with a great service that fills a particular niche, and yet she's probably throwing money out the window by talking herself out of sales on a regular basis.

Based upon my own personal experiences with sales training programs I've been through, I think most training is at the root of this massive problem. Every course I've taken has gone through the steps of a sale and they teach salespeople to go through each and every step. The problem is, what if all the steps don't need to take place? For example, "objection handling" is always taught as one of the steps of a sale. But what if the prospect doesn't have any objections? When I called that company I just mentioned, I'd already passed the "objection handling" stage simply because their web site had done a thorough job of handling my objections. When I was working for that one company I mentioned earlier, simply taking the calls that came into my line as a result of my personal marketing program, many of those prospects had no objections because my marketing program had taken care of them in advance. By assuming that each of these steps are going to take place, a lot of salespeople will cause something to happen when it really shouldn't have to to begin with. If a prospect doesn't come up with any major objections, don't give them a reason to. It's like shooting yourself in the foot with a really big gun!

I've seen a lot of companies and managers require their reps to fill out a "lead sheet" or something similar that documents each step of the sale. This assumes that each of the steps will happen when they may not. If you're required to maintain these types of records, skip anything that doesn't happen naturally. Don't force a prospect to enter a selling phase that may not only be unnecessary, but may cause you to lose the sale entirely.

Use the KISS test when you're selling. Before every action you take with a prospect, ask yourself if you're keeping it simple or if you're throwing monkey wrenches into your machinery. Believe me, you'll save yourself a lot of wasted time, headaches, and lost sales by doing so. I did.

## LEARN TO QUALIFY-OUT

Another principle that's difficult for most salespeople to accomplish is the idea of not merely qualifying prospects, but of qualifying them out. This is something that gets easier with experience. As for me, once I'd built a self-marketing program that was working, I had been in sales long enough to hear every excuse and to recognize every signal that someone wasn't serious or was only out to waste my time or try to get something for free. Early on, it's a lot harder to pick these people out, and it's especially difficult to decline to meet with a prospect who is requesting an appointment with you.

The problem is that unqualified prospects are the single biggest time waster for salespeople. Nothing is more frustrating than being excited about getting a lead and an appointment, only to get out there and find out that they're not serious or are not capable of buying or paying your price. I went through that repeatedly early on, and even though other, more experienced salespeople kept trying to drill the idea of qualifying out into my head, I was just too afraid to do it. To complicate matters, this was before I had figured out how to generate quality leads. I was still cold calling, so leads were definitely few and far between, and I rationalized that going out to meet with a prospect who may or may not be qualified was better than not having anyone to meet with at all. In reality, this wasn't a solid argument simply because having no appointment is actually better than having an unqualified one. If you have no appointment, your time is free to spend on finding qualified prospects. If you've gone out to an unqualified appointment with a prospect who will never buy, you've wasted your valuable time, and remember, time is our most precious resource.

In order to be able to effectively qualify prospects out, you must prepare yourself in advance and condition your mind through the principles explained in the chapter on power. Now, the flip side to this is that attempting to qualify a prospect out definitely places you in a position of tremendous power, probably more so than anything else you can do!

Most prospects are used to needy salespeople who act desperate and will do anything to get in front of them and try to get a sale. As soon as you start asking questions in an attempt to qualify them out, you instantly become more desirable to work with and the prospect has a natural tendency to want to buy from you. This is because of the principle of scarcity and the natural tendency of humans to want what they cannot have or what is less available. Nobody wants to buy from a desperate salesperson, but everybody wants to buy from someone who appears to not need their business, and who even goes so far as to require the prospect to show why they should be allowed to meet with that salesperson.

There's a term I've heard called the "wanting-it tax." The wanting-it tax simply means that the more you obviously want something, the higher the price will go. Think of what it's like to buy a car. If you test-drive the car, become very excited about it, and make it clear that you really want the car, the salesperson or manager is going to be far less willing to negotiate. People who sell cars for a living are taught this principle, and know that if someone is drooling all over a car, they'll eventually give in and pay the full sticker price, no matter how much they try to negotiate at the start. The opposite is also true; if you drive the car and act unimpressed, and even point out some flaws that you've noticed, car lots will tend to immediately drop the price and tell you what kind of deal they'd be willing to do. At this point, power has shifted and the wanting-it tax is now working against the salesperson. Because they want the sale more than you want the car, or at least appear to want it, they'll start making concessions. The same is true in any sales situation. Whoever wants it more is going to pay more. If you make it all too clear that you want and need the sale, the prospect will be entirely unwilling to pay a fair price. On the other hand, if they clearly need what you've got and you avoid acting too excited, and even convey an image that you are already prosperous and don't need their business, they'll be a lot easier to work with and more willing to pay a higher price. This is why I don't recommend that salespeople say a lot of commonly heard things like, "I'd really like to earn your business." In fact, that salesperson I mentioned earlier who always talked himself out of sales always said this, and prospects immediately started making him jump through hoops for them. The wanting-it tax applies as soon as you say anything like that.

The actual process of qualifying prospects out is nonspecific and depends entirely on your particular offering and what makes a prospect either qualified or unqualified to buy it. I give you an example from my days of selling business telephone systems. Once my self-marketing system was operating in full force, I had a constant flood of calls and e-mails coming in. As one would guess, most of them were from small businesses and mom-and-pop shops who were in need of a phone system. A typical scenario was someone who needed three or four phones for a small office. Since I was working for the highest-cost provider at the time, and because business phone systems are expensive to begin with, a system of that size equipped for a few lines cost at least $2,000, and that's without voice mail or any other add-ons. So my main qualifying-out question was, "What budget have you set for this purchase?" or, "How much are you looking to spend?" About half of those calling would answer the question. If they said a few hundred dollars or a thousand dollars, I simply told them they'd be looking at at least two thousand dollars, and asked if they were still interested in meeting. Most weren't. As for the other half, those who refused to answer because they thought I was trying to find what their budget was just so I'd know where to set my price, I simply said, "You're looking at $2,000 at a minimum, without the cost of wiring, voice mail, or other features." That effectively qualified out those who weren't even close to budgeting that amount for a phone system.

By contrast, most of the other reps in the office immediately ran out to every new lead they came across. In fact, this got to be a source of humor and entertainment over time for the more experienced reps! When I became one of the experienced ones who was mentoring entry-level reps, I told them about qualifying out, but just like me when I was starting out, they didn't listen. They ran out to every lead they got, and two out of three times they came back disappointed because the prospect either had no money or flew off the handle when they saw the price. Just think of all the time and money they wasted by driving around and burning up gas on unqualified prospects.

Another aspect of qualifying out is that it provides you with valuable information you'll need in order to justify spending your time with this prospect, as well as information that will be helpful during your first appointment. There must be what is known as a "trigger event." A trigger event is something that creates a need, which in turn requires the prospect to buy. In the phone business, this was usually a new location, a move, or an expansion. In the life insurance business this is usually a marriage or the arrival of a first child. In any case, without a trigger event, the prospect will have no compelling reason to buy and probably won't. Even prospects who think they want to buy will usually back out and decide not to make a purchase if there is no trigger event taking place. For example, when I came across a prospect that was opening a new location or moving to a larger building, I knew they'd have to buy a phone system, and they always did, regardless of whether I got the sale. On the other hand, prospects who wanted to meet and get a proposal because they felt their phone system was getting old and were possibly interested in getting a new one almost never bought. They had no real trigger event. Once you learn that a trigger event indeed exists, you can go ahead and consider the prospect qualified, and you can also use that information to better prepare yourself for the first appointment. You should also find out what the prospect's time frame is. If they have a trigger event and a real need but it isn't going to take place for a year, you'll probably want to suggest meeting at a later date. Be tactful and polite about this, and give reasons why it's not in the prospect's best interests to meet so far in advance. Plans change, and so on. Just don't come off like you aren't interested in anything that you won't get paid on right away.

All you need are a few powerful, direct questions that you can use to effectively qualify the time wasters out. Mine were based upon price and trigger events. Figure out what you can ask to qualify prospects out in regard to your product or service.

Another aspect of qualifying out has to do with making sure you're dealing with the real decision maker and not a go-between. This is crucial, because the single biggest reason sales aren't closed is because the salesperson was dealing with the wrong person all along. I was guilty of this big-time during my first few years in sales. To me, it was just too difficult and even risky to always work on getting to the correct person and to avoid appointments with those who weren't ultimate decision makers. It was risky because I was still in the mindset of simply getting appointments. Be very careful not to fall into this trap. One of the biggest fallacies of traditional sales training as well as management has to do with the fact that salespeople are encouraged to get as many appointments as possible, and to set daily and/or weekly goals for appointment setting. This is another reason why I'm against the old activity-planning model of "multiply this by that and the other thing." In my case, I was under pressure from managers to set X number of new appointments, not to mention the pressure I put on myself, so when I got an appointment I didn't even bother to screen the person I was to meet with in order to find out if they were making a decision or if they were just collecting proposals for the person who really would be.

The problems with meeting with the wrong person are many and go beyond the obvious fact that if you don't meet with the real decision maker, all of your sales talent goes right out the window and the decision will be made based only on the proposals. In most cases, a decision maker who is handed a stack of proposals goes straight to the pricing pages and buys the cheapest one. All of the hard work you put into preparing for your appointments, finding and addressing needs, presenting and closing, becomes irrelevant.

One of the biggest challenges in dealing with a nondecision maker has to do with what these people are looking for compared to what a real decision maker is looking for and what you are striving to achieve. This goes back to the three main business goals. While an owner or executive cares only about those important goals, an office manager, for instance, might be overly concerned with the color of the product or how many bells and whistles it has or how that person can use it personally. As soon as the owner sees the proposal, however, and realizes that it addresses no real goals, it will go straight into the trash, or a decision will be made solely on price. Another problem with dealing with a nondecision maker has to do with the fact that they typically have way more free time on their hands than a real decision maker does. They will waste lots and lots of your time because meeting with a salesperson is the only chance they ever get to exercise any authority. They also tend to look for freebies, such as lunches or anything else they can milk out of you and your expense account. In this era of downsizing and right-sizing, more people than ever are trying to justify their jobs, and a nondecision maker with too much free time will request more and more detailed information, graphs, pie charts, technical data, white papers, references, testimonials, and on and on, just to look busy. In the end, if you don't meet with the real boss, he or she will buy solely on price or won't even buy at all, and all of your time and effort will have been wasted.

The worst part about dealing with these people is that they can't make a decision. All they can do is hand your proposal over to the real decision maker. You then have no way to do your job—sell—and your chances of getting the sale drop dramatically. Avoid this mistake at all cost, and always deal with the real decision maker.

## GETTING THE FIRST APPOINTMENT

Getting the first appointment is self-explanatory. If you're dealing with an interested prospect who has passed your qualifying-out screening process, they'll naturally want to meet with you.

In spite of that, I bring the subject up for a couple of reasons. The first one has to do with The KISS Test. Although appointments are usually necessary, sometimes they're not. Even in the phone system business I sometimes closed sales via fax without ever having met with the customers. When I was selling telecom and Internet services later on, I never met with at least half of my customers, and this was in an industry where most sales managers have a mandatory two- or three-appointment requirement when it comes to their sales process, complete with the intricate lead sheets I mentioned earlier. To this day I'm still amazed at how many of those companies went bankrupt and how you can trace the causes straight back to the sales department and all the silly rules imposed upon the salespeople by ineffective and frequently inexperienced managers. When I was selling Internet service, I would sell half of my customers via fax or e-mail with no in-person appointments while I routinely watched those around me losing sales and annoying people who were simply trying to buy by insisting that they set an appointment and meet in person. Don't do this.

The other point I want to bring up regarding appointment setting has to do with coming from a position of power and control. Again, approach this using the principles in the chapter on power. By first trying to qualify a prospect out, then creating an impression that the opportunity to meet with you is a privilege, you're setting yourself up to maintain complete control over the sales process and get the sale in the end. Think about the concept of the prospect having to gain your acceptance as to why you should meet with them, and choose a time to meet based upon what is convenient for the salesperson first and for the prospect second.

## PREPARING FOR THE INITIAL MEETING

In preparing for your initial appointment, there are a few things you need to research and have in order in advance. They are:

- General information about the company if you're meeting with a business. The best place to find this is online by simply searching under the company name. Check their web site as well for recent press releases, new product releases, expansion announcements, new locations, news of buyouts, mergers, additional funding, and so on.
- A clear idea of why you're going there and what the prospect's immediate need is. You should have obtained this information in your qualifying-out process when you found out what trigger event is taking place that is causing the prospect to buy. If you didn't, you're not doing a thorough enough job of attempting to qualify prospects out, and if you're meeting with a prospect who has no trigger event, you're probably wasting your time anyway. Once you have this information, you can mentally rehearse what you'll talk about during the appointment, what specific questions you'll need to ask, and what detailed information you'll need to obtain.
- A clear idea of what the prospect's time frame is. This is important not only to qualify out prospects who have needs too far in the future for you to spend time on now, but also because you'll need to be prepared if the prospect has an immediate need that must be addressed right away. I frequently came across prospects who were moving into a new building but hadn't bothered with buying a phone system until the last minute and needed an expedited order. Because there were additional fees and paperwork associated with expedited orders, it was important for me to know this in advance so I could be prepared and have the necessary paperwork ready on the appointment.
- Materials you'll need to bring with you. This may be pricing, brochures, demo equipment, samples, and so on. I frequently encountered prospects who needed to see demo phones or who wanted samples of the various colors available, and if I didn't have this prepared in advance, I'd have to run out there a second time and extend my sales cycle in the process.

Once you have all of this information together, you need to start thinking about what your strategy with this particular prospect will be. Since you know what the prospect's need or trigger event is, and since you also have a good idea of what their time frame is, you'll be able to position yourself from that point of view and mentally rehearse what you'll talk about and exactly what kinds of questions you'll need to ask. To get an idea of what I'm talking about, consider time frames. If you're going out to meet with a prospect who has a need but who does not intend to make a purchase right away, you'll want to avoid talking about how good you are at delivering your product or service lightning-fast. Likewise, if they need it right now, don't talk about how thorough and meticulous your company is regarding delivery or installation. While these are great virtues, they'll convince someone who is in a hurry only that you'll miss their deadline.

Aside from the obvious fact that it gives you what you need to close the deal, going in with a strategy that is particularly relevant to each prospect serves to differentiate and set you apart from your run-of-the-mill competition. Ninety percent of salespeople will go in, ask all the same questions, and follow the same sales process, otherwise known as the steps to a sale. They'll even fail to use The KISS Test and will try to force prospects through steps that are entirely unnecessary and that will waste everyone's time and needlessly lengthen the sales cycle. When you're direct and to-the-point in a way that speaks to each prospect's particular situation, you'll have a tremendous advantage over your competition.

## A RELEVANT QUESTIONING PROCESS

In addition to knowing the specific information relevant to your prospect prior to a first appointment, you must also have a clear understanding of what your first appointment objectives will be. You can then derive your questions from each objective you'll need to accomplish in the appointment. Here is a general list. You should customize this list for yourself and your products or services, but in most cases, each point is relevant:

- Establish and maintain control of the sales process in a positive manner. This means of course that you operate from a position of power and authority and establish control so that you can steer the sales process in the right direction. If you do not establish and maintain this control, the fate of your sale will be left to the prospect's whim, and you'll fall into the old routine of delayed decisions, unreturned phone calls, and a general inability to get the deal closed. In addition, you also establish yourself as a business equal, which builds the prospect's confidence and creates the feeling of a business partnership rather than a sales situation.

- Find common ground. By finding common ground, I don't mean an attempt at rapport building where you're simply trying to find things you have in common personally. What I'm referring to here is recognizing and identifying with the prospect's ideals, or more specifically, helping the prospect to identify with your ideals. You need to do this in a way that comes off as genuine and not contrived. This requires excellent listening skills, something that is necessary for success in sales anyway, and the ability to pick things out that the prospect says and relate them to the ideals and goals of yourself or your organization.

- Establish time frames. You did this in your preliminary, qualifying-out call with the prospect. Now you want to get definite time commitments from the prospect. If you're involved in a more complicated or longer sales cycle, establish time frames for each of the various steps you'll need to go through.

- Continue to qualify. Here, you'll want to continue to ask qualifying questions. The reason is twofold. First, you want to make absolutely sure that this prospect is for real and truly has a need and intends to buy. If they get wishy-washy or contradict some of their affirmative answers to your earlier qualifying-out questions, be on guard. The other reason is to advance your sale. By further qualifying prospects and having them give positive answers to your questions, you're effectively helping them to overcome many or all potential objections, and therefore can accelerate the sales process and shorten your sales cycle.

- Gain trust and confidence. You do this through your professionalism, your image that you and your organization can get the job done, through your status as a business equal and your position of authority, and through your ability to get right down to the prospect's real needs and to address them directly.

You also do this by listening more than talking. As a salesperson you must always focus on asking, questioning, and probing, not on talking.

- Position yourself for the long term. You need to make it clear that you and your organization will be there to serve the prospect's needs and do whatever you can to ensure their satisfaction. Be careful here: Telling boring company stories and making empty promises isn't the way to accomplish this. You must be especially careful to avoid saying things like, "We want to be your business partner." Such statements insult prospects' intelligence. If you were a true business partner, it would be in your best interests to provide your products or services for free! This rule can be a double-edged sword if you're not careful; the key is to let them know that you're pursuing a long-term business relationship—not a partnership—rather than a one-time sale.

- Establish your credibility. Your credibility is built on many of the previous guidelines, such as instilling trust and confidence, qualifying the prospect in a relevant manner, making it clear that you're in it for the long term, and conveying your status as a business equal.

- Establish credibility in your company/products/services. Once you have credibility with the prospect, your organization must obtain that credibility as well. In many cases, this is assumed, and you won't need to put much effort into this. On the other hand, if you don't have name recognition behind you, or if you're a startup venture without a reputation and list of clients, you'll have to be absolutely certain to establish credibility, or your competition will convince the prospect to write you off as a "here today, gone tomorrow" outfit.

- Be ultraprepared. This is one of the surest ways to guarantee that you'll remain in control of the appointment and the sales process in general. If you're not prepared, you'll be caught off guard by the prospect's questions and you'll immediately lose your credibility in addition to control. Never show up for an appointment without first having the information I talked about, and never go into an appointment without reviewing these objectives and mentally rehearsing what you'll say and do to attain them.

• Gain commitment for the next step. It is imperative that you never, ever walk out of an appointment without gaining the prospect's commitment for the next step. If the prospect refuses his or her commitment, it's a pretty good sign that they're not serious and a sale may not take place. (This is another albeit somewhat indirect form of qualifying.) If your next step is a second appointment, set the date and time. If your next step is a site visit, set the date and time. If your next step is a demonstration, set a date and time. If you've already closed the sale, they're off the hook; however, give your commitment to the prospect as to when you'll follow up and how. Always have your appointment book or PDA with you. Without your calendar at hand, you obviously can't set appointments while you're out in the field. Keep one thing in mind about gaining commitment for the next step: Never ask the prospect if you may call them. I'm referring to the line that all too many salespeople blurt out when they're leaving an appointment, which is, "Can I call you next week if I don't hear from you?" Of course a prospect is going to say no! If you ask and they say no, then you definitely can't call them. If you do, you haven't kept your word and you've violated their trust, which serves to negate all the positive things that have been listed here. If you don't ask, you don't give the prospect a chance to say no, don't call, so you're free to call or not call. If you don't hear from them in a week and you call, everything will be fine. If they said no, don't call, and you call, you've probably just annoyed the prospect and greatly reduced your chances of getting the sale. One of your more patient, less-needy competitors will get it.

These guidelines will enable you to develop a series of standard questions that will allow you to achieve these objectives, accelerate your sales process and avoid stalling, and save a lot of otherwise wasted time.

Another thing you need to know in order to develop a powerful questioning process is to know what not to ask. Salespeople are unfortunately trained to ask many questions that are not only irrelevant but often serve to offend and even anger prospects, or give them reasons why they should not buy. Here are some guidelines as to what questions you should never ask, unless any of them happen to be directly relevant to your product or service:

- Vague, generalized questions about the prospect's business. In typical sales training programs, we're instructed to ask such things as,

  "What are your main goals?"

  "Where do you want to be in five years?"

  "Who are your main competitors?"

  These questions usually have absolutely nothing to do with what you're selling. Never, ever ask them unless they are directly relevant to your product or service; for example, a commercial loan officer attempting to close a five-year business loan would certainly need the company's five-year business plan. For everyone else, avoid asking for this information at all cost unless there is a real need to know. I can clearly remember several appointments where I launched into these dumb questions and the prospect gave me an equally vague answer, along with a blank look as if to say, "What does this have to do with _____ ?" Even more vividly, I can remember prospects telling me that it's none of my damned business, and even getting angry and asking me to leave. One of them told me to become an investor in the company and then and only then would I be permitted to view such highly confidential information.
- Questions about the company's operations that have nothing to do what you can offer them. A good example here is another typical question that telecommunications salespeople were always taught to ask:

  "Do you have people working out in the field, or traveling to and from the office?"

  While this would be relevant to someone selling cellular telephones or business phone systems, it only annoyed people who were looking to save money on their long-distance service or get Internet access or a computer network in the office. They took the attitude that I was incompetent and was only wasting their time, and they were right.
- Irrelevant personal questions about the prospect or about anyone else within their organization. This has to do with the fact that

empty, personal rapport building is to be avoided, and also has to do with the fact that such questions are usually considered to be intrusive. They're also important to avoid because they don't serve to provide any of the information you'll actually need in order to put together a solution for this prospect. The exception here is if you're selling personal services such as insurance and the information you're seeking is absolutely relevant and necessary to your sales process.

- Questions that serve to affirm the prospect's satisfaction with their current provider and therefore give them reasons not to buy. This has to do with the following series of questions that many traditional training programs instruct salespeople to ask:

  "What do you like about your current provider?"

  "What do you dislike about your current provider?"

  "What would you change about your current provider?"

  While the latter two questions make sense for a salesperson to ask, the first one probably causes more sales to be lost than I'd care to even think about. If you're a prospect and you're considering a change, you not only need to have reasons to justify bringing in a new provider, but you also need reasons to get rid of your current provider. The moment you ask a prospect what they like about their current provider, you immediately cause them to think about all the good points their current provider has, all the things they've done right, and all the reasons why the prospect should keep them. You really hurt your chances of getting a sale. By only allowing the prospect to focus on what they do NOT like about their current provider, and what they would change, you not only reinforce the prospect's belief that they need to change, but you also have something to work with in putting forth your reasons as to why you can serve their needs best.

## GET YOUR PROFIT-JUSTIFICATION INFORMATION

Profit justification is the most powerful thing you can do to convince a prospect to buy from you, usually at the full price, and close the deal. Profit justification is the only way of writing proposals and presenting that speaks directly to, and only to, the three main business goals that every prospect needs to accomplish or improve upon.

Profit justification simply means showing the prospect how your particular product or service will put more money into their pocket. The three main goals, and how they relate, are as follows:

1. *Increase revenues.* This is the one thing that every business always wants to accomplish, with no exceptions whatsoever. Everyone would like to make more money regardless of whether they're a business or an individual. In some cases, this is a direct and obvious benefit derived from your product or service. An advertising salesperson is a great example. The sole purpose of advertising is to get more people to buy. Increasing advertising spending therefore increases incoming revenues. A financial services representative shows individual clients how they can invest their money and grow it over time. With some other products and services, the benefit isn't so obvious but it's still there. It takes a bit of digging and thinking on your part. When I sold phone systems, I always looked for applications that would allow customers to increase revenues. I might find flaws and problems in their system that resulted in long hold times for callers who eventually hung up as a result, and showed the prospects how they could utilize certain features to process calls more efficiently and prevent people from hanging up. A typical example of how I profit-justified a solution looked something like this:

| | |
|---|---:|
| Calls per day | 50 |
| % of callers who make a purchase | 25% |
| Average revenue per sale | $100 |
| Est. number of hang-ups per day | 12 |

12 lost calls × 25% = 3 lost sales
3 lost sales × $100/sale = $300/day in lost revenue
$300/day × 20 business days = $6,000 lost every month

| | |
|---|---:|
| Monthly payment on new system | $1,500 |
| Additional monthly revenue recovered by new system | $6,000 |

$6,000 – $1,500 = $4,500 more income per month
$54,000 more income per year

As you can see, this is a direct financial benefit for the prospect that they can realize only by installing the new, up-to-date system. Almost none of the salespeople I worked with used this strategy. First of all, if you don't go into profit justification fact-finding, neither you nor the prospect will ever know how much revenue they're losing. Without this knowledge, most prospects will fly off the handle at the thought of paying out $1,500 month for a new system. Because they can't see all the money they're losing and how the new system would recover this money, they see the $1,500/month as a straight expense. If I didn't profit-justify my solution, I'd lose the sale to the low-cost provider who is quoting $800/month, which really is a straight expense because their salespeople never profit-justified anything or solved any real problems for the prospect. By profit-justifying the solution, all they see is the $4,500/month coming in as increased revenues. The $1,500 payment isn't a payment anymore; it's an investment that will automatically triple itself each and every month.

This example is something I commonly did to get large sales closed. My competitors came in talking about how great their companies were, how long they've been in business, who their big-name customers are, and about all the great new features and technology their systems had. It's pretty easy to see why I never lost a sale when I presented in this way and spoke directly to the decision maker's real requirement for increased revenues.

2. *Decrease expenses.* This one is self-explanatory. It's all about saving the prospect money. If you look at commodity sales such as long-distance service, most Internet services, and competitive power services, the only reason people usually ever buy any of them or change providers is because of price. Long-distance service is long-distance service; the dial tone on the phone line is always the same regardless of who the provider is. It's only about price.

If you're a low-cost provider, it's perfectly fine to sell on low prices. In fact, for a low-cost provider, that's probably your entire business strategy, and that's fine. The problems begin when people who aren't low-cost providers start trying to sell on price. There's an old sales saying that goes, "If you live by price, you die by price." This is so true because if you try to sell on price, then you must really have the lowest price, or you have no chance of getting the sale. As soon as you start talking about low prices and saving money, you immediately convince the prospect that they're going to buy the cheapest price. Ninety-nine percent of the time they're going to shop around a bit before buying from you, and if somebody else has a lower price, they'll find it and you'll be shut out.

If you're not the lowest-cost provider, you need to avoid selling on price like the plague. Your job is to find ways that you can sell on points one or three—increasing revenues or increasing efficiency/profitability. Even if you're selling a commodity product, come up with creative ways to justify your solutions on something other than price or you'll be facing an uphill battle and a low close ratio.

If you are the low-cost provider and you're selling on price, always break your savings out so the prospect can see exactly how much they're saving. If you're going to save them $100/month on something, also add a line item showing $1,200/year in savings. You always want to make the most impact, and yearly savings are always far more dramatic than just monthly savings. This is especially true with a business prospect, since they tend to look at the big picture rather than just the short-term.

3. *Increase efficiency/profitability.* This is a fairly easy point to sell on, especially to a business customer. Time is money in the business world, and if you can save someone time, you're also indirectly telling them that you can save them money, and you don't need to show actual numbers like you do in straight profit justification; however, in some cases it makes sense to break the numbers out.

Let's say an office manager is wasting two hours per day on mundane tasks that your product can automate, and let's say this same person is paid a salary that breaks down to $20/hour. Time is money, and by wasting two hours a day, the company is effectively wasting $40/day on manpower. A profit-justification breakdown might look something like this:

| | |
|---|---|
| Time Mr. X is spending per day on this task | 2 hours |
| Mr. X's time is worth | $20/hour |
| Wasted manpower per day in dollars | $40 |

| | |
|---|---:|
| Wasted manpower per month | $800 |
| Monthly payment for this piece of equipment | $200 |
| Manpower effectively recovered | $800 |
| $800 recovered – $200 payment = | $600/month |
| | or $3,600/year |

Although this example refers to a piece of office equipment, the product doesn't have to be tangible, and in fact intangibles are sometimes best justified in this manner. A recruiter can profit-justify services by showing how much of the boss' valuable time is saved. An accountant can show not only how much time will be saved by not spending it on tedious tax returns, but can also show the possibility of increased revenues through a potentially larger tax refund.

Aside from examples using actual dollars, many prospects have a real desire to simply make their lives easier. This equates to increasing efficiency, and if you can prove to someone that your product or service will accomplish this, you've effectively demonstrated point three on the all-important list of main business goals.

## UNCOVER THE PROSPECT'S REAL NEED

Uncovering a real need can be extremely challenging. Many prospects are reluctant to reveal their real needs because of possible embarrassment or because sensitive information is involved that cannot be revealed, or that the person simply isn't comfortable talking about.

A perfect example has to do with the fact that as technology increases, many tasks that have always been handled by people can now be automated. This frequently came up in the phone business as business owners sought to have automated attendants and menu-driven systems answering incoming calls. In many instances, they wanted this equipment in order to decrease expenses by laying off one or more employees. Because they couldn't reveal this information for fear of the soon-to-be-fired employees finding out, or simply because of a moral dilemma with the situation within themselves, it was sometimes very difficult to figure out the real need behind a prospect's desire to meet with me.

While profit justification is applicable almost all of the time, there are cases where a prospect has a personal desire and that's the only reason they're looking to buy. Even in the phone business I encountered the occasional customer who just wanted lots of flashy high-tech features.

Aside from that, a number of prospects simply aren't willing to take the time to allow you to develop a relevant proposal that will enable them to make an intelligent decision. In those cases, you can either qualify them out, move on to the next prospect, or simply put together a proposal based upon the little bit of information you do have and quote your lowest possible price. While you might get a sale this way— I did on occasion—the chances are slim and you don't want to spend much time on these deals. In these cases, the prospect's real need is usually price, and your best shot at getting the sale is to quote the lowest price you can.

## KNOW THE DECISION MAKING PROCESS

One of the most crucial pieces of information you must obtain, either on the phone ahead of time or during the first appointment, is the prospect's decision making process. This means knowing that you're with the correct decision maker or makers, and also knowing what other requirements and what information the prospect will need to have before they can make a decision. Some examples of things that are commonly overlooked are:

- Customer references or testimonials.
- Equipment demonstrations.
- A meeting or call with an outside consultant, additional vendor, or contractor whom you'll need to interface with.
- A tour of your facilities by the decision maker.
- Assistance with obtaining financing.
- Meetings or demonstrations with other people in the company in addition to the decision maker, such as employees who will actually be using the new product or service.

Like so many other things in sales, some of these items can be a double-edged sword if you don't approach or handle them correctly. For instance, if a prospect isn't using any outside consultants, don't bring it up and give the prospect the idea that maybe they should, which will lengthen the sales cycle and put you in danger of losing the sale, since so many consultants are heavily biased. What you need to do is ask the prospect who else will be involved in the decision making process and ask to have those people included. You also need to ask what other requirements they'll have or what they'll need to see before making a final decision.

Part of this is also establishing a time frame for your sale. You first need to find out when the prospect wants or needs your product implemented. You then need to ask them when they expect to make a final decision. If you're selling something that takes 60 days to deliver or implement and they plan to make a decision 30 days ahead of time, you need to find out now and to let them know about it. If you don't, you'll have a very angry prospect and a possible cancellation on your hands when they find out they can't get their needs taken care of in time.

Finally, don't jump the gun and irritate the prospect by calling and asking if a decision has been made in advance of the date they've committed to making a decision by. Few things annoy prospects as much as this, simply because 99 percent of salespeople do it. Avoid it and you'll differentiate yourself from the competition even more.

# 20

---

# DEVELOPING
# A RELEVANT
# AND POWERFUL
# PROPOSAL

## ALWAYS REMEMBER THE PROSPECT'S REAL NEED

One of the most common mistakes salespeople make is to present a proposal that contains a vast amount of information that's totally irrelevant to the prospect's needs. How many of us have included information on our company's financial strength, time in business, noteworthy clients, and our CEO's bio? Most of us have done it without realizing that prospects never read any of it.

With that in mind, always try to refrain from including lots of information that you or your company considers important but that has nothing to do with addressing the prospect's real needs and giving them reasons and justification as to why they should buy from you.

## THE PROCESS OF PROFIT JUSTIFICATION

Profit justification is the centerpiece of a powerful proposal. The process of profit justification begins during the fact-finding process, through your questioning. You'll then take this information back to your office with you and use it to find ways to demonstrate that your product will increase revenues, decrease expenses, and/or increase efficiency/profitability. It culminates in a proposal that shows the prospect, in hard dollars, exactly how you'll do this and how much you'll make for them or save them.

The trick in profit justification is actually uncovering problems and associating them with actual dollars. There is a common questioning process used in sales that just touches on the concept but falls short of putting it into terms of real dollars. It uncovers problems but it stops there. You may use it or may have used it in the past. It goes something like this:

"When _____ happens, what problems does that cause?"

"And what problems does that cause?"

"What does that lead to?"

"And what does that result in?"

And on and on. It does an excellent job of making prospects realize that what may seem like a small problem or mere annoyance really does cost them money, but it fails to put a dollar amount on that loss.

In looking for opportunities to find hard-dollar losses that you can use to profit-justify your proposal, you need to think backwards. Take each of the three main business goals and reverse them as follows:

### *Increase Revenues*

I've already mentioned certain types of sales, such as advertising for businesses or investing for individuals, that directly increase revenues (or money in general). These are simple to profit-justify because it's clear that the end result of a purchase will be increased revenues, and you can easily come up with hard dollar amounts based upon past performance of your products or services.

In most cases, however, you'll be showing them how much money your product or service will recover. In other words, you're showing them how you can stop losses. To prove that you can stop losses, you need to find losses. So the first step in showing that you can increase revenues is to look for places where the business is leaving money on the table. In my example in the previous chapter, I showed the prospect that my solution would prevent buyers from getting stuck on hold and eventually hanging up the phone without buying something.

The process of finding losses that you can fix begins exactly like the example I gave of a common questioning process that serves to find problems but doesn't put a dollar figure on them. What you need to do is begin with the same or a similar series of questions, but direct them to finding real dollars. This is where it becomes very important to maintain control over the situation, and your image of power and high business status are especially critical here.

Because your questioning process in using profit justification will be so different than the usual salesperson's fact-finding questions, it's a good idea to give the prospect a heads-up so you don't catch them off guard. Chances are, they've never had any salesperson go into such an intelligent, thorough questioning process, and they're expecting the status quo sales appointment. What I like to say is, "I do things a bit differently from most salespeople, but I do it because I'm almost always able to find ways and means of developing solutions that can actually improve your operations and put money back into your pocket. I may ask a few questions that probe into information that is considered sensitive or confidential to you. If I do, just let me know and we'll move on." Prospects appreciate this because they won't feel like you're being nosey and intrusive when you start digging deep to look for problems, and they won't be uncomfortable with telling you something is confidential and cannot be revealed if you happen upon anything that is.

A conversation with a prospect using that line of questioning and then directing it toward finding hard dollars might go something like this:

*Prospect:* The biggest problem we've had with our current supplier is that they've been consistently late recently, and it causes problems.

*You:* What specific problems does that cause?

*Prospect:* Well, when they deliver late, my staff can't get the next weeks' worth of inventory ready to go. It's a real inconvenience.

*You:* Yes, that would be an inconvenience. What happens as a result of not having your inventory ready?

*Prospect:* When the inventory isn't ready, it goes into backorder status and the retail stores that carry our products run out of stock and get very upset with us.

*You:* They run out of stock? For how long?

*Prospect:* Usually about two days. That's been the typical situation lately as far as these guys being late.

*You:* Two days. How much product does each of your retailers usually move in a week?

*Prospect:* Hmm . . . well, I'd say each of them averages about $1,000 a week. They're not big stores but they add up when you put them all together.

*You:* A thousand a week? Times all those stores? That's a lot of money! Two days is almost a third of the week. Being conservative then, is it safe to say that being without product for two days a week is hurting your revenue stream by about 25 percent?

*Prospect:* Yes, that's definitely a fair and conservative number. Sometimes it can go longer than that.

*You:* Okay, great. For the sake of example, I like to be conservative, so we'll go with 25 percent. Twenty-five percent of $1,000 is $250 a week. How many retailers are affected by this?

*Prospect:* We have about 30 in all.

*You:* Bear with me for a minute here while I add this up. Okay. If you have 30 stores and this issue is causing a loss of $250/week per store, you're losing about $7,500 a week. Is that close to being accurate?

*Prospect:* Yes, in fact based upon my own estimates that's very accurate. Of course the number changes each week but that's a good average figure to work with.

*You:* Okay. So $7,500 a week roughly equals $30,000 a month, all because XYZ Company can't get their deliveries in on time?

*Prospect:* Yes, it makes me very angry; we've been with them so long and I like them personally, but this is simply an unacceptable amount of money to lose because some of their new staff happens to be lazy.

*You:* Well I'm glad we were able to identify this problem. Tell you what: Let's set a time to meet a week from tomorrow. I'm going to talk with some of the people in my office and see what we can come up with that might solve this for you.

Get the picture? It's really easy once you get the hang of it! Ask the right questions and maintain control so you can steer the conversation in the right direction.

Many salespeople are uncomfortable doing this when they first see it done and the first several times they try to do it themselves. They're afraid prospects will be unwilling to reveal this sort of information about money and their internal operations. In reality, prospects are usually thrilled when you start asking these kinds of questions. It communicates to them that you are thinking like a business owner and not like a salesperson. They're sick and tired of salespeople who come in and talk about their company story and the latest features that nobody else has but who are unable to identify and address real business needs.

Keep in mind that these aren't the generic, irrelevant questions that will anger prospects, like asking them what their five-year goals are or who their five biggest competitors are. These questions bother prospects because they're totally irrelevant to the situation at hand and because they're obviously taught to salespeople as a generic set of questions to ask in the absence of anything else.

The key is to keep asking the right questions until you land on hard-dollar figures that you can use to close a sale. Most salespeople who haven't been trained in profit-justification techniques would start with the same first question, but the conversation would go something like this:

*Prospect:* The biggest problem we've had with our current supplier is that they've been consistently late recently, and it causes problems.
*You:* What specific problems does that cause?
*Prospect:* Well, when they deliver late, my staff can't get the next weeks' worth of inventory ready to go. It's a real inconvenience.
*You:* Mr. Prospect, I can certainly understand your frustration there. Let me reassure you that this is something you will never experience with ABC Company. We've been in the business for more than 15 years and we have a stellar customer satisfaction record. I can provide you with a list of our better-known customers. They're all very happy with us. We've never been late all the time like your supplier is. Let's get you started with our services. Would you prefer plan A or plan B that we discussed earlier?
*Prospect:* Well . . . I'd really need to think about it first. I've been with XYZ Company for a long time, and despite what you say, I have no real way of knowing that you'd be any better. I have to take the

time to think about whether I'd really want to sever my relationship with them.

*You:* I can assure you that you won't have those problems with us. We have the best service and support in the industry.

*Prospect:* Well, I do like them personally so let me first see if I can work this out with them, and to be quite honest I'd need to see exactly how and why you'd be better rather than looking at a list of who your big customers are. In fact, that worries me because I'm sure you take care of your big customers first over someone like me.

*You:* That isn't the case; we treat everyone with equal importance, but since I would love to show you how and why, let's meet again next week.

*Prospect:* I'd prefer not to set a time now. I'll call you when I make up my mind.

*You:* Okay, no problem, I'll just give you a call if I don't hear from you.

*Prospect:* No, don't call me, I'll call you.

And with that, it's over. In fact, instead of getting the prospect excited and worked up over all the money you might potentially recover for him, the conversation escalated into a conflict that killed any chance of a sale or future relationship. This is why it's SO important to get valuable profit-justification information and to use it to build a proposal that will not only get the prospect's attention but will make them want to sign right now! I'm willing to bet that 9 out of 10 salespeople do things just like the second example shows. I know because I used to do it, too. The moment the prospect mentions a problem or something they'd like to change about their current provider, the salesperson jumps right in about how their company can do it so much better and that the prospect should buy for that reason. This fails to go far enough; you need to show the prospect why they need to switch or to add your service or product in terms of real dollars. You especially need to avoid talking about how your company or how your product's features can solve some of the problems they're experiencing, and yes, in many cases that's something they need to know, but only after you have all your information in hand, have organized it into a proposal, and are in front of the prospect for a presentation and closing meeting.

### Decrease Expenses

Even though this one is easier to show on paper, again you must think backwards. If you're trying to help them decrease expenses, you first have to find out where they're spending too much and exactly how much.

In many cases, you'll need a copy of a bill or invoice or will at least need to get the prospect to tell you how much they're paying. This isn't always easy; many prospects consider this information to be confidential, or they'll withhold it and simply ask you to give your best price.

There are some creative ways to decrease a prospect's expenses while accomplishing both of the other goals as well. When I was selling phone systems, I frequently met with companies who were paying huge monthly bills for their old, antiquated phones under the old phone company rental plans. In many cases, I was able to provide them with the latest technology for a lease payment that was less than their existing monthly payment. In addition to directly decreasing their expenses, I also found applications where they could use the new technology to increase both revenues and efficiency/profitability. That is the ultimate win-win situation!

When it comes to finding ways to decrease a prospect's expenses, I highly recommend finding ways to accomplish at least one of the other two business goals. This is because of the reality that "If you live by price, you die by price." There's always a chance that someone will undercut you or offer to match your price, and if price is all you had, you just lost the sale. However, if you can help the prospect achieve other goals in addition to cutting costs, you'll be the favorite to get the sale.

### Increase Efficiency/Profitability

Showing how a prospect can increase efficiency—and therefore profitability—can go way beyond just showing them timesaving features or explaining how your services can make their lives easier.

Because recruiters are one group I've worked with who usually aren't trained in profit justification and who have difficulty seeing how they can use it in a hands-on way, here's a sample conversation that might take place between a recruiter who is attempting to sell her services to a small business and the owner of the company. Observe how the questioning process begins innocently enough, then is carefully directed toward hard dollars:

*You:* As I briefly mentioned on the phone, we specialize in finding and screening highly qualified candidates for the job openings that come available as your company expands and turns over existing employees.

*Prospect:* Yes, I've never worked with recruiters before and I'm not familiar with how you work, but it's really been time-consuming to go through resumes and conduct interviews and background checks, especially when few of them turn out to be anything close to what I'm looking for.

*You:* Yes, I remember you mentioning that on the phone. Exactly how much time does that take up?

*Prospect:* I'd say a good 10 hours a week. It may not sound like much but it's putting too many other projects on hold. I'm here only about 50 hours a week so that's a big chunk of my time.

*You:* Yes, it certainly is. That would come out to 20 percent, a lot of time for anyone. By the way, what kind of projects are you working on, if you don't mind my asking, of course?

*Prospect:* There's a new product line I'm trying to roll out. I've done the research, and the market and demand are definitely there. It's just a matter of finding the time to move forward with it, not to mention the fact that I can't even consider doing it until I have the additional staff to handle all the extra work, phone traffic, and customer service issues that will naturally result. I'd love to jump in and do it myself, but I have a family and a promise to myself to not work the long hours that too many business owners work.

*You:* It sounds pretty significant. I take it this new product line will be a major portion of the company's revenues?

*Prospect:* Yes, in fact I've done quite a bit of test marketing on the Internet and I'm conservatively estimating that the new line will account for a 50 percent increase in our overall revenues once it's rolled out.

*You:* Wow! I read your company information on your web site, and if I remember correctly your current revenues are at $60,000 a month?

*Prospect:* Yes, that's correct. Nice job!

*You:* Thanks! Business really interests me, and I hope to own a company as well in the future. But a 50 percent increase over $60,000 will equate to $90,000 a month in total revenue. Now that's impressive.

*Prospect:* Thank you. Now you can see why it's so important to me to get this hiring out of the way and to move forward. It's also extremely frustrating to me that it's not getting done, but as I've already mentioned, my commitment to my family comes first.

*You:* That's great. I can totally appreciate where you're coming from there. Let me make sure I understand your underlying need then. When I came out here today it was under the assumption that you simply need some extra help, which of course would mean additional employee expenses for you. But in reality, these new hires will actually be an investment in your new products that will result in an extra $30,000 a month, or $360,000 a year for you?

*Prospect:* You've got it. Finally, someone who understands what I'm talking about instead of bragging about how big their staffing company is!

*You:* Thank you! The way I see it, my job is to help my clients because that's what will make me successful in the end. By the way, keep in mind that not only will we find the talented staff to get your project rolling, but we'll drastically reduce the time you're spending on resumes, interviews, and so on. Since all you'll be involved with are the final interviews with the very best candidates, that 10 hours a week you're now spending should go down to about 2, and only for a couple of weeks at that. Based upon your revenues, your time here as the owner has to be worth at least $1,000 dollars a day.

*Prospect:* You can say that again. I not only have a responsibility to myself and my family but to my employees, who rely on me for a paycheck and benefits. Spending time on nonproductive activities costs everyone money.

As you can see, this conversation found two definite areas where hard dollars can be added to the business's bottom line. First, there's the new product line that will be worth an extra $30,000 a month. Then there's the owner, whose time is conservatively valued at $1,000 a day, or $20,000 a month. This is a tremendous amount of money, and it allows the executive recruiter to easily justify her high fees, fees that at least seem high to anyone who has not had a profit-justified proposal presented to them. They won't seem high to this prospect. In fact, they'll seem like a ridiculously small investment considering the substantial returns they'll result in.

Think about how a recruiter who was not trained in profit justification would have handled this situation. It would have been a conversation about how they're the best company, how they'll find and produce the best job candidates, how they'll be easy to work with, and so on. However, this approach fails to find those hard dollars that are music to the ears of a business owner or executive! Remember, always think like a business owner. That one line in the conversation where the prospect said how much he appreciates the fact that the salesperson was thinking like a business owner wasn't made up. I had several people tell me that, once I had learned how to do this. In fact, you'll begin to make some very powerful contacts and form several beneficial business relationships as a result of using these techniques. Once you start putting money back into people's pockets using these techniques, you'll be seen as a trusted confidant and business advisor, and your customers will continue to come to you for advice in all areas, not to mention provide you with endless referrals. This also serves to make you the most desirable networking partner anyone can have, and that in turn leads to even more quality leads.

The most important thing about this example conversation is that the salesperson managed to uncover the prospect's real, underlying need. The outside appearance was a simple need to find good candidates to fill some open positions. The real need, however, was much more important than that. It was about giving the prospect what he needed—in this case, time and people—to get a major project started, a project that would result in spectacular profits. Always tactfully direct your questioning to find that real, underlying need, because more often than not, there is one and it's not easy to see.

## FULFILLING THE THREE MAIN BUSINESS NEEDS

Now that you've accomplished the task of using powerful questioning to uncover the prospect's real need and to gain the all-important information you'll need to prepare a highly relevant proposal that will profit-justify your solution and address those real needs, you'll need to figure out how you're going to present this to your prospect.

Before you decide upon how you're going to present your solution and demonstrate your profit justification, think back to your appointment(s) with the prospect, and think about what kind of person he or she is. People tend to be one of the three following types:

- *Visual.* The visual personality type gains understanding through seeing. For these people, the use of visual aids in your proposal is key. Flowcharts, graphs, and PowerPoint presentations may be important, as well as photos of the product itself if you're selling something tangible. You must show them instead of simply telling them. While this isn't always the case, you can frequently pick these people out by their words. They commonly say things like, "Get the picture?" or "Can you see it?"

- *Auditory.* The auditory personality gains understanding through listening. If you're dealing with an auditory, communicate your message verbally. They'll be bored by visual presentations. Keep the visual aids to a minimum and plan to communicate your message to this person through speech.

- *Kinesthetic, or "touchy-feely."* I've always found these personality types to be the most difficult of the three to communicate effectively with, for me anyway. They communicate and perceive information emotionally. These are the people who commonly say things like, "I like your proposal but need to make sure everyone else feels good about it." These are the people who may want to make a purchase based upon their own personal desires rather than sound business motives. Also, if you're selling something tangible, definitely bring a sample product or invite the prospect to a hands-on demonstration if you're dealing with a kinesthetic. Letting them put their hands on the product is one of the best ways to get them emotionally committed to buying, in many ways like a test drive convinces many people to buy a new car.

Speaking of test-driving a car, think of how each of these three personality types would interpret and be moved by a test drive. The visual will lovingly admire the lines of the car for a while before and after driving it. A visual will also continually scan the interior of the car and take in as much of it as possible, and may be moved by the textures and depth of materials. An auditory might enjoy the sound of the engine under acceleration, will play with the sound system to see what it's like, or will even drive with the radio off and the windows closed to check the noise level. A kinesthetic will pay attention to how the car feels—what the steering and brakes feel like, how the ride quality feels, how comfortable the seats are, and so on. A touchy-feely will also be more emotionally swayed by trivialities like new car smell.

Using this information about what kind of person you're dealing with, decide what methods you'll use to convey your message to the prospect. Once you do that, you'll know exactly what you'll need to do to create the perfect proposal to motivate this person to buy!

## OUTWARD APPEARANCE

The outward physical appearance of a good proposal needs to be professional, clean, and straightforward. By straightforward, I mean you should avoid handing the prospect a three-ring binder with 100 pages of information and white papers in it when all you need is a few pages of product information, a few pages of profit-justification information, and a pricing page. When I started out selling phone systems, I assumed every prospect would want every last bit of technical data on the equipment, so my proposals were heavy three-ring binders with a good 200 pages of information. I stopped doing this when I noticed that almost every prospect did the same thing upon receiving it: They turned to the Contents, found out where the pricing page was, skipped everything else, and went straight for the price. By putting so much information in there, I guaranteed that nobody would read any of it and would go right for the price. A few of our sales reps would try to be cute by doing the 100-page proposal and conveniently leaving the pricing page out, which they'd hand to the prospect only after they'd gone through the entire proposal. As you might guess, this infuriated busy decision makers who had neither the time nor the inclination to thumb through so much irrelevant information, and few of those sales were ever won.

As time went on, I began using simple pocket folders with the company logo printed on the front and my business cards attached to the inside. I say cards because I always included a few extras, just in case anyone else would be involved with the decision whom I didn't know about in advance, and also with the hope that the prospect might pass them on to anyone whom I could be of service to. In the left pocket I included product brochures, photos, and any other information that might be necessary in making a decision. I was careful to avoid any company story brochures and kept mine to the exact products I was proposing to the customer. In the right pocket were a few pages consisting of the profit-justification portion of the proposal, a pricing page, and contracts that were already preprinted and needed only the customer's signature to move forward with an order.

Another aspect of the physical appearance and feel of your proposal has to do with the prospect's personality type. Is she a visual, an auditory, or a touchy-feely? If I'm dealing with a visual, I'll go heavy on charts and graphs in the profit-justification section of the proposal, include product brochures that have a particular emphasis on photographs and diagrams, and maybe even include one of the interactive CD-ROMs that the company produced. I also brought demo equipment along when I was dealing with a visual. I didn't plug it in or actually demonstrate it; I simply left a phone sitting on the desk, and would notice how visuals always stared at it throughout the course of the conversation.

When dealing with an auditory, I kept the graphs, charts, and photographs to the bare minimum. I used just enough to make my point, but not so much as to distract or bore the prospect. I focused on communicating my message verbally. In other words, there wasn't much in the way of pictures or actual products, just a lengthy conversation with detailed explanations of everything I was trying to communicate.

When it came to touchy-feely types, I again avoided too much in the way of pictures and graphics, but definitely brought out the demo equipment. In the case of a touchy-feely type, I brought the actual demo kit, plugged it in, and turned it on. I'd preprogram features ahead of time that were relevant to what the prospect was looking for, or that were associated with the profit-justification solution I was proposing. Touchy-feelies would get all excited and carried away playing with the equipment and trying out all the new features. Especially since few of my competitors went to the trouble to do this, it was extremely effective in closing sales.

In organizing the information that will actually go into your proposal, you should base it upon the prospect's requirements as to what they'll need to make a decision. Follow the instructions in the chapter on the sales appointment process where you make absolutely certain not to overlook any crucial pieces of information they will require to make a final decision.

Depending on what the prospect's real, underlying need is, there are several possibilities as to what your proposal will focus on. Here are some common scenarios that you'll run into often:

### *Profit Justification*

This is the one you should always be striving for in your appointments and fact finding. When you hit on solid profit-justification information, run with it and make that the centerpiece of your proposal and your entire sale. Nothing makes a sale easier to close than profit justification, and it applies to individuals as well as to businesses.

A friend of mine owns a company that paints houses with a new, high-tech ceramic coating paint that is not only guaranteed to last at least 20 years, but that acts as such a good insulator that it reduces heating costs in the winter and air-conditioning costs in the summer. This is easily profit-justified, especially in cases where the customer is financing the purchase. The savings on utility bills more than makes up for the monthly payment in a lot of instances, and therefore a loss has been recovered and money has been put back into the customer's pocket. There's also profit justification in the fact that most people paint their houses every 5 to 7 years, while this is guaranteed to last at least 20. This is profit justification in the "reduce expenses" column. I provide you with this example to show that profit justification can be used just as effectively with individuals and consumers as with businesses or other organizations such as governments, churches, and nonprofits.

Keep your profit justification as simple and to-the-point as possible without leaving any pertinent information out. When showing a profit justification of increased revenue, I always preferred to do mine in a flowchart format so the prospect could see how the problems within their organization flowed, exactly how each problem triggered more problems, and how one or more of those problems led to hard-dollar losses.

If you're profit-justifying an increase in efficiency/profitability, you can do the same flowchart format, but in a simplified manner that relates to what peoples' time is worth and how you'll recover lost man-hours and put the money right back into the business' bottom line.

Profit-justifying a decrease in expenses is the simplest of all, and simply requires a few line item entries just like some of the examples I've already shown.

### A Personal Need, Want, or Desire

If the prospect's real need turns out to be nothing more than a personal want or desire, simply focus your proposal on how your solution will address those needs. Personal wants are usually feature-related, and this is the one time where it's okay to talk about features and make that the focus of your presentation.

If you're selling something that may include both profit justification as well as a personal need, include both. Start out with your profit justification and focus on that because that's what makes the most impact with a prospect. Remember, pain or joy felt in terms of dollars usually makes the deepest and most lasting impression. Let's say you're an accountant, and someone inquires about services in order to simply save time and avoid the hassle of going through boxes full of receipts and completing tax returns on time. If your fact-finding reveals that you can recover quite a bit of money for this person, either in the form of a lower tax payment or a higher refund, talk about that first. Then you can point out that on top of putting money back into the prospect's pocket, you'll also make that person's life much easier and free their time up for more important things like family.

In presenting a solution to a personal need or desire, stick with the guidelines regarding the three main personality types. Even if you're selling an intangible, you can relate your product to the various types. For example, even though a mortgage is an intangible instrument represented by a mere piece of paper, mortgage brokers put pictures of beautiful homes on their web sites and brochures. This is because those beautiful homes relate directly to a visual's mode of receiving communication.

### A Must-Have Purchase

If someone is buying something only because they need it, or as a replacement for something that is old and worn out, keep your proposal simple and demonstrate how your product or service will meet and exceed their requirements.

Common examples of must-have purchases are office equipment for a new business location, a new home for a newlywed couple, furnishings for a new home, additional staff for a business, and so on.

As always, look for opportunities to profit-justify, regardless of why they may be meeting with you to begin with. If you do a good job of questioning, aren't afraid to ask those questions, and dig deep enough, you can almost always uncover something that you can use to at least partially profit-justify your proposal.

## AVOID CLICHÉS AND USELESS INFORMATION

Again, don't inundate the prospect with lots of irrelevant information that will have absolutely no effect on their decision. Company stories, financial data, the CEO's bio, and bragging about big-shot clients come at the head of the list. Nobody cares, nobody will read it, and in fact many people will be turned off by it. Remember, all the prospect cares about is the prospect. That's it. The fact that your CEO won an Entrepreneur of the Year award is not going to sway them to choose you over your competition.

I'm also very careful to avoid typical sales clichés in proposals. Including them is equivalent to failing to keep the proposal strictly relevant to the prospect and their needs. Some typical sales clichés are:

"We have the best service and support."

"We provide the utmost in customer satisfaction."

"We've been the fastest-growing company in our industry for the past three years."

And on and on. Avoid them! Remember, prospects care only about themselves, and unless you can show what you'll be able to do for them and only them, your chances of getting a sale are slim to none.

# 21

## PRESENTING YOUR PROPOSAL AND GETTING THE SALE

### PREPARATION

Preparation for your presentation includes a number of things. They are:

- Knowing your prospect's personal style and personality type. You'll know this from your experience with having had one or more prior appointments with this person. Everyone falls into either the visual, auditory, or touchy-feely type. Some people can be a combination of two.
- Who will be present, how you'll present to a group if there will be one, and whom you'll most want to focus your attention on. It's also a good idea to know who is what personality type in the event that you'll be presenting to multiple people. If you're presenting to a CEO who is an auditory and a COO who is a visual, you'll need to satisfy both.
- The layout of the prospect's office, conference room, home, or wherever else you'll be meeting. This is important because it may limit your options as to presentation tools. You wouldn't want to prepare an overhead or PowerPoint presentation only to present in a small, cluttered office that has no room to accommodate it.

- A very clear understanding of what the prospect's real needs and trigger event(s) are and how you'll address them. Review your proposal beforehand and mentally rehearse this part of your presentation. Remember, stick to the facts; it's easy to get sidetracked and throw in some information about your company or your impressive list of clients despite the fact that none of it is in your proposal and has nothing to do with satisfying the prospect's real needs.
- Preparing yourself and your own personal image. You have to look sharp and be sharp. Overdress and get a good night's sleep the night before your presentation. Eat a light lunch if your presentation is in the afternoon; otherwise you might feel fatigued. On the same note, don't drink too much coffee or otherwise overload on caffeine or you'll be jittery and appear nervous to your audience.

## KNOW WHOM YOU'RE TALKING TO

When I say know whom you're talking to, I mean know who in the room are the real decision makers and influencers, and who will have nothing at all to do with the decision. Furthermore, know what each individual person's needs are, and direct the various parts of your presentation to the correct people to make sure their needs are being addressed.

A good example of this goes back, once again, to the phone business. In most cases, the owner of the company made the final decision as to which phone system they would buy. However, many owners were smart enough to have the receptionist sit in at meetings and participate in equipment demonstrations. This was for the simple reason that the receptionist would have to live with the new equipment more than anyone else. Salespeople who only talked to the owner and who effectively ignored the receptionist lost sales. This is because any business owner knows that if the receptionist isn't comfortable with the equipment and won't be able to use it effectively, it will be a disaster waiting to happen, no matter how great your profit-justification numbers are. There are a lot of cases where more than one person will participate in meetings but the salesperson focuses only on the boss and fails to acknowledge other influencers' needs. This is a grave mistake, so make sure you don't do it.

Part of the process of knowing whom you're talking to is setting yourself up in the proper physical orientation to present to all the important people who will take part in the decision. Place yourself and your presentation materials in a position where everyone has an equal view of you and is within earshot, and vice versa. You want to be able to communicate well with everyone in the room, especially as questions come up along the way that you'll need to address.

Finding out who will be involved with the decision making process is something you should always strive to do on the first appointment or even prior to that on the phone. If you don't, you'll be caught off guard when presentation time comes, and you won't be prepared to address each person's needs and get the sale closed.

## DON'T BORE THEM—STICK TO WHAT'S RELEVANT

I cannot stress enough just how important it is to stick exactly to what is important to the prospect. This means avoiding all the usual pieces of a presentation that, for some reason, are almost always included despite the fact that they have absolutely nothing to do with the prospect's needs. Remember, prospects care only about themselves and their own needs. They don't care about you and your company and how great you are.

Things to avoid:

- Company story. I don't think I've ever seen a presentation that didn't include a company story or general company information. The fact is that you wouldn't have been invited back for a presentation if the prospect wasn't comfortable with the company. Once I figured this out for myself, I became frustrated simply because every last one of my managers—with one notable exception—required all of us to include company stories in our proposals, and to always tell the company story during the presentation. Sometimes I was even forced to bring out a flip chart with endless pages about the company and the management, and prospects' eyes would always glaze over as I went through it. By the way, the one notable exception as far as managers was the same one who first confirmed my suspicions that cold calling doesn't work. He conducted his own training on a regular basis for us, above and beyond the standard company training, and one of those classes in particular still stands out in my mind today. He had shown us the results from a survey of a large number of business owners asking them what they dislike most about salespeople, or what is the one thing they'd change about the way salespeople conduct themselves. The number one complaint from business owners was the company story. They collectively said that it's entirely irrelevant, has zero influence on their final decision, and in fact is frequently perceived as arrogant on the part of both the company and the salesperson. I can't think of any better reason to avoid company stories than this!

- Company financial data/statement of financial strength. This is similar to a company story. The difference is that even a lot of salespeople who understand that a company story is harmful still believe that they have to prove to the prospect that they're financially stable and will be in business long enough to serve the prospect's needs. Unless a prospect specifically asks about this, don't bring it up. It's boring and has zero influence on a prospect's decision in cases where the prospect didn't ask for it. I personally believe that talking about your company's financial condition actually has the effect of raising doubts and suspicions about the company's financial health. It's like an old joke I heard about Honest Jack's Car Sales. The fact that he's calling himself honest implies that he's a crook! Companies that place too much emphasis on trying to prove that they're financially solvent only raise doubts about their financial health.

- Information on product features that aren't directly relevant to your proposal or the prospect's needs. This mistake was always difficult to avoid in the phone business because the latest equipment was always full of amazing, high-tech features that we naturally assumed prospects would get excited over. However, I learned over time that once I addressed the prospect's needs, whether it was through profit justification or something as simple as giving them specific features that they asked for, telling them that what they were going to buy had all these other great, dazzling features didn't accomplish anything. In fact, it managed to scare a lot of them out of buying. By talking about all these extras they were getting that had absolutely nothing to do with the real focus of the proposal, several prospects got the idea that they'd have to spend hours and hours studying thick manuals just to be able to use the thing. This reminds me of an article I read not too long ago about some of the new, high-end luxury cars. Apparently they're so full of technology that doing something as simple as changing the radio station may require scrolling through menus on an in-dash computer screen, and buyers are being scared away by it. This is the same exact thing that happens in the mind of prospects when you start rattling off everything their new purchase will be able to do. Only speak directly to the prospect's real needs. Once you've addressed and satisfied those needs, get the order signed. If you really want to show them all the great stuff they're getting, wait until after their purchase is implemented.

- Customer references that the prospect didn't request. Another thing that always annoyed me about some of the companies I worked for was that on top of requiring a company story, they required us to include standard lists of references with all our proposals. They rationalized that by including them up front, prospects wouldn't have to ask for them and therefore lengthen the sales cycle. This argument isn't sound for a couple of reasons. First, intelligent prospects generally don't ask for references. They know full well that if they ask, you're going to give them only the names and numbers of your very happiest customers who would entrust you with their very lives. Nobody is going to include an unhappy customer, and nobody is going to hand over a random list without first calling those people to confirm that they're happy and that they'll give you a stellar reference. Second, by including a generic list that everyone uses, you run the risk of alienating the prospect. What if the people on your reference sheet are not at all similar in nature to this particular prospect? Or what if the opposite happens; what if you're proposing to a Fortune 500 company but there are no others on the list? They'll assume you don't have the capacity to handle their demanding requirements. What if you're selling something to a mom-and-pop store and your list is full of larger companies? What if you're selling services to a lower-income individual and your reference sheet is full of names on the rich side of town? It's too easy to create an impression that you specialize in catering to a certain kind of prospect that is too dissimilar from the one you're attempting to close.

- Case studies in unrelated industries. Case studies can be some of the most powerful selling tools around. If your product or service has done wonderful things for ABC Company or Mr. and Mrs. X, and a case study has been prepared showing exactly how, when, and how much was accomplished, that sometimes can be all it takes to get an undecided prospect off the fence. The problems begin, however, when you're providing case studies for industries or scenarios that have nothing at all to do with the prospect at hand. If you're selling to a school, you're not advancing your cause by including a case study about how you saved lots of money for a car dealership. You're not helping by showing a wealthy individual how your financial products pulled someone out of poverty. Case studies can alienate prospects just as quickly and easily as reference sheets that list people in totally opposite situations.

- Any generic information that has nothing to do with the issue at hand. This really goes back to my suggestion early on that you avoid attempts at empty, personal rapport building unless the prospect initiates it. In a presentation meeting, everyone involved—especially the final decision maker—is anxious to get right down to business and hear your presentation and, of course, finally learn the price. This is the worst possible time to make an attempt at useless small talk that won't get you any closer to a sale.

## PROVE THAT YOU CAN MEET THEIR REAL NEEDS

This is the proverbial "do or die" part of the presentation. Now you're finally going to be face-to-face with the decision maker. Your opportunity to present the powerful information and proposal you've developed is finally here.

This presentation appointment must hit on a number of important steps. They are, in order:

1. A review of why you're there in the first place. Briefly run through the reasons the prospect agreed to meet with you to begin with and what their initial need or concern was. This is also a good time to touch on any points the prospect made as to why you might be the best choice for them. For example, if you're local and the prospect mentioned that it's important for them to deal with someone locally, quickly remind them of that. (Always jot these things down as they come up.)

2. A review of the information you gathered and uncovered during your fact-finding process. Here is where you're going to run through everything you and the prospect talked about during your

first appointment. This is to refresh the prospect's memory and remind them of why they need to make a purchase. This is also to gain the prospect's agreement on each point. You should start out by saying, "I'd like to briefly run through what we talked about last time just to make sure I have everything correct before moving forward." Then as you make each point, gain the prospect's acceptance by simply asking, "Is that correct?" or "Do I have that right?" Not only are you verifying that you really do have everything correct and as it took place, but you're helping the prospect to solidify their desire and need to make a decision to buy.

3. A presentation and explanation of the profit-justification facts you uncovered and developed, preferably through the use of a flowchart. Here you'll actually turn to the profit-justification flowchart you've created and take the prospect through it, step-by-step. You're showing them not only what you've developed, but continuing to gain the prospect's acceptance of each point by having them confirm its validity. This really drives each point home and has the effect of further solidifying their decision to go ahead and buy.
   and/or,
   If this sale does not involve profit justification but rather focuses on the prospect's literal needs or desires, you'll run through each of those needs and confirm that they are, in fact, the things that, if satisfied, will mean that your solution is the right one.

4. A presentation of the profit-justification financial analysis. This is where you'll present those line items, hard dollar figures that are the culmination of a good profit-justification sales presentation. This is where the prospect will see exactly how much money you're putting back into their pocket in the form of increased revenues, how much money you're saving them in the form of decreased expenses, and how much money you're either recovering for them or saving them, in addition to the intangible benefits, derived as the result of an increase in efficiency and therefore profitability.
   or,
   A presentation of exactly how your solution addresses each and every one of the prospect's important needs and desires. Go through them, one by one, in much the same line item fashion that a profit-justification proposal goes through each hard dollar

amount either made or saved for the prospect. Explain exactly how and why your solution will take care of all those needs and desires.

5. An explanation of what's necessary to move forward. This is simply where you tell the prospect what they need to do next, for example sign an order, fill out paperwork, give you a check or credit card, and so on.

6. Ask for the order. Few sales will be closed unless you ask for the order. I prefer not to literally ask someone to buy; instead, it's better to be subtle and low-key about it. "Let's get you started on this" is one of my favorites. It's also fun and effective to add some urgency with an embedded command such as "right now." An embedded command is simply a command that you embed within a sentence or paragraph that tells a prospect to do something, but without coming right out and saying it. So, for example, instead of saying, "You can expect installation a week after you place your order," I like to say, "When you buy right now, we'll go ahead and schedule your installation for a week from today." This also works very well in sales letters and even on web sites.

Thank the prospect and help them to solidify their decision. Never leave without sincerely thanking the prospect. This is simply out of common courtesy. Part of the money they're spending is going straight into your pocket in the form of commission, so you owe it to the prospect—now your customer—to thank them. In addition, I think it's a good idea to help them solidify their decision in their mind and let them know they did the right thing. You don't accomplish this by saying it directly. In fact, saying, "You made a great choice" will sometimes even raise doubts in the customer's mind. Instead, ask your new customer why they chose you over the competition. They'll then give all the reasons, which usually consist of how much they like you, how much they like the product or the company, or how you and your solution will accomplish exactly what they wanted and will do a lot of good. In other words, this causes customers to further sell themselves on the purchase they've already made.

## PRODUCT DEMONSTRATIONS

Many presentation and closing appointments will involve product demonstrations. Because few prospects are willing to take time out of their day to come to your office, you'll almost always have to do this on the prospect's territory.

The important thing is to make sure you have everything you need in order, and arrive early! Any number of things can go wrong with an equipment demo. If it normally takes 10 minutes to set up, get there 20 minutes before your scheduled appointment time. While you're at it, be sure to let either the prospect or someone else who will be involved know that you'll need to arrive early in order to get set up.

Be prepared for any eventuality. I learned this the hard way when I was doing phone system demos. It didn't take many instances of not having a power outlet anywhere near where the demo was supposed to take place for me to buy a long extension cord and keep it in my car. Think of anything that can possibly go wrong and keep the solution in your car at all times.

These same rules apply to any presentation tools you'll be using. If your presentation will include a projector, easel, or flip chart, arrive early so you can set up on time, and keep any accessories or tools you might need if something goes wrong in your car.

## FIND OUT WHAT COMES NEXT

Finding out what comes next is important if you intend to do a good follow-up, which you must do if you want your customers to be happy and to provide you with a steady stream of referrals.

This has to do with implementation, coordinating with anyone you need to coordinate with, and so on. In many cases, once a sale is closed, there are outside third parties whom you'll need to interface with to make things happen. Never leave the meeting with a signed order unless and until you go over this with your new customer. I distinctly remember having people calling and screaming at me because the implementation of what I had sold was causing them big problems, which could have been avoided if I'd simply asked the customer who would be affected during the installation process and how we could work together to minimize problems.

## IF THEY DON'T BUY RIGHT AWAY

If you don't get the order on your presentation appointment, don't give up just yet. Although this system of selling is designed to minimize objections, they do happen, and you can overcome them. There may be some internal bureaucracy that must be dealt with on the prospect's end, or you may simply be dealing with someone who has a policy of not buying anything without sleeping on it first. Whatever the reason, all is not lost just yet, unless of course they flat out told you no!

The key here is to find out why and what is going to happen next, or what specifically is causing the prospect not to buy. Some common reasons are:

- They're not convinced yet. If a prospect is not yet convinced that your solution is the way to go, you can usually overcome this on the spot, assuming your proposal is strong enough. If your proposal is weak and doesn't strongly address their needs or solve one or more problems, you need to go back and do a better job of creating the proposal. Simply ask the prospect what, in particular, is giving them cause for concern. There's a good chance they simply missed or misunderstood something in your proposal or presentation, and you can easily go back and go over it again to make sure they understand. There may be a number of things they're unsure of. Some people are slower than others, and other people need to see something repeatedly before it hits home. If this is the case, be patient and understanding and continue to go through the material until your prospect finally sees why they should go with you. At that point you can ask for the order again.

- "We need to think about it." Whenever someone says this, I assume it's an excuse and they simply don't want to step up and make a decision. Here's my response to that line: "Great, I can certainly understand that. Just to make sure you have all the information you'll need to make an informed decision, what in particular about this do you want to think about?" If they don't give you an answer, there's a good chance that it's just a blow off and they don't have the courage to say no to your face. You may want to cut your losses and move on if that happens. However, if they do give reasons—and most do—you can now address them one by one and go back to asking for the order. Once you've addressed their needs, there's obviously nothing left to think about and you can go ahead and use your justification information to reinforce all the reasons why they should go ahead and buy from you.

- They just can't make decisions. Let's face it; many people are weak and have no ability to make a decision. I eventually added the following quote from Napoleon Hill below my e-mail signature: "The man of DECISION cannot be stopped. The man of INDECISION cannot be started. Take your own choice." This is such a good point because people who are either unable or unwilling to make decisions never amount to much. If you're dealing with one of these people, think about whether this is someone you really want as a customer. We've all had problem customers who definitely weren't worth the commission we made from the sale. You may very well be dealing with one. If you've done everything correctly and have properly presented compelling reasons as to why the prospect should buy from you, and they won't offer up any real objections or things they want to think about or consider, you may be facing that most dreaded of all prospects, one who cannot make a decision no matter what.
- They can't afford it. This is a tough one because no one wants to admit it. The only time anyone usually comes out and says this is if they're bluffing and simply trying to get a better price. Many times, a prospect who cannot afford to buy will come off like someone who cannot make a decision. If they can't afford it, there's nothing you can do but move on. Hopefully you'll weed most of these people out early on in your qualifying-out process.
- They won't buy right away on principle. Many people have a personal policy of never buying anything right then and there, and always sleeping on it first. If this is the case, relax, because you have nothing to worry about. Your proposal was based upon solid, good, definite reasons to buy and not on irrational emotion. Just carry yourself with confidence and convey the message that you know they'll buy.

In any case, remember that few sales are lost just because a prospect didn't buy on the presentation appointment. As I said, many people just want to sit on it for a day before moving forward. Whatever you do, don't start harassing your prospects and keep asking them when they intend to make a decision. This is annoying and insulting, but unfortunately, a majority of salespeople do it, anyway.

# 22

---

# FOLLOWING UP AND KEEPING YOUR CUSTOMERS HAPPY

## THANK YOU

I've already mentioned the importance of thanking your new customers at the close of the appointment. In addition, be sure to send out a thank-you card. E-mail is acceptable and it's what most salespeople are using nowadays but I don't think it's enough; a handwritten note is far more personalized and appreciated by prospects.

If you're selling big-ticket items, something a little more impressive might be in order, such as a gift basket or gift certificate to a nice restaurant. When you're selling big-ticket products or services, the prospects know you're making a substantial commission, so be sure to show your appreciation for that.

## OBTAINING REFERRALS

Obtaining referrals from your customers is one of the single most important things you can do to ensure your sales success, yet few salespeople do it or approach it correctly. Some don't bother, others don't think of it, and still others fail to do so out of a lack of confidence, because they think this will upset customers, or that it's somehow inappropriate. Nothing could be further from the truth.

Remember when you asked the customer why they bought from you? This not only reassures the customer that they've made the right choice, but also sets them up to willingly give you some great referrals. Because buying from you was such a great experience and will result in tremendous benefits, it's only natural for them to want to recommend you to others like themselves.

There are several key times that are especially great for asking for referrals. They are:

1. Immediately after you close the sale. Right after you close the sale, and especially right after you ask the customer why they chose to buy from you, is probably the best time to ask for referrals. This is because the customer is relieved to have made a decision, is therefore probably more relaxed, and because by asking them why they bought from you, they're even more comfortable with you and with their decision and will definitely be more willing to offer up some great referrals.

2. Immediately after installation or implementation. This is another time when the prospect will be at ease, because another big burden has finally been taken care of. They're usually happy and excited to get started with their new purchase. When you call following installation, delivery, or implementation, whatever the case may be, ask for referrals once you've confirmed that the prospect is happy and satisfied. If for some reason there was a problem and things didn't go so smoothly, you must do everything in your power to correct the situation and make the customer happy. Once you do this, many prospects will be thrilled that you handled the situation so well and will happily offer up referrals.

3. When you follow up down the road. I'm going to advise that you keep in touch with your customers for the long term. This is a good idea even if a customer retention or after market rep is assigned to the customer after you've closed the initial sale (this is common in many companies that follow the hunter/farmer system in which salespeople either prospect for new business only or work existing customers, but not both).

## OBTAINING TESTIMONIALS

Obtaining a testimonial from a happy customer is one step better than getting referrals. Of course, I always ask for both with an exceedingly happy customer. When it comes to testimonials, there are two types that will be of use to you: One is a regular testimonial letter, on the customer's letterhead, telling the story of what a great job you did of meeting their needs and exceeding their expectations. The other variety is simply a "one-liner," or a simple quote. These are great because you can use them on all of your various marketing materials. When a prospect sees something like, "ABC Company was able to find and correct losses and put $5,000 a month back into my company's bottom line," signed by one of your customers, it goes a long way toward increasing the effectiveness of your marketing pieces. Remember to use these everywhere!

As for a regular testimonial letter, I like to carry those with me. Put them in protective sheets and carry them in your planner or binder. Testimonial letters are also really great for use on your web site. You can scan them and either include links to them on your site or put them right on a Testimonials page. They really go a long way toward increasing the response rates you'll receive and generate even more prequalified leads for you.

## KEEP YOUR CUSTOMERS UP-TO-DATE

I think it's very important—in fact, I think we have a responsibility—to keep our customers up-to-date on the newest, most recently available products and services that might be of benefit to them. They really appreciate it when you work to keep them well-informed of anything that might help them.

The other obvious benefit is that if you stay in touch and keep them up-to-date on the latest and greatest, they'll be a lot more likely to buy from you again. Existing customers can be some of the most valuable in terms of repeat business, so never forget them! One of the biggest mistakes I made for a long time was that I was so preoccupied with generating lots and lots of leads that I started to neglect my existing customers and lost a lot of potential business as a result. Remember, your existing customers have already put money into your pocket, so you owe it to them to keep them updated.

## YOUR CUSTOMERS-ONLY NEWSLETTER

You've already seen how exceedingly powerful an e-mail newsletter is for generating a very high volume of very well-qualified leads. Why not use the same idea to keep your customers up-to-date? Think about it; Not only is a newsletter great for getting prospects, but it's also great for really conveying a personal touch to your existing customers. If you send out a monthly customers-only newsletter, they'll always remember you, they'll contact you with referrals, and they'll contact you to buy more. A newsletter takes your customers and keeps them in prospect status indefinitely!

I think the number one reason that customers don't come back for repeat business and offer more referrals is simply because they forget about the salesperson. By keeping your name in front of them on a regular basis, in exactly the same way that your prospect newsletter keeps your name in front of prospects, you'll start hearing from your customers when they have another reason to buy or when someone they know can use your services.

# 23

## FINAL THOUGHTS ON MODERN SELF-MARKETING

### IT'S BASED ON PROSPECTING, BUT THE ENTIRE SYSTEM IS DIFFERENT

Hopefully by now you've gained a clear understanding of the fact that when you get people to call you instead of you cold calling them, the entire sales process changes. There is a totally different dynamic at work, and if you sell the way I advise, you'll get the biggest possible advantage out of it and close far more sales than you ever thought possible.

Remember, when you put yourself in the position of someone who can truly help prospects and who is a real business equal, you'll experience a whole new world of selling. The old days of chasing prospects and routinely getting the run around will be over.

### MAINTAIN THE RIGHT ATTITUDE AND PERSONA

The key to maximizing your results is to always maintain the right attitude and carry the ultraconfident persona through right to the end. When you're first learning these techniques, it's very easy to slip right back into your old way of doing things, so be careful not to. It's important to always work on your new image and persona of supreme confidence and to come back to this information often to refresh your memory and look for ways you can improve.

## BUILD ON YOUR SYSTEMS

Because self-marketing efforts are cumulative, your results will continue to increase over time, to a point where you have more leads coming in than you know what to do with! Of course, when that happens, you can be really selective about qualifying and work only with those people who are ready to buy, right now.

It's important to implement and use all of the various self-marketing techniques you now have at your disposal. By doing so, you'll gradually build each individual system into your master system of systems. Be sure to keep things organized; it's easy to let everything get out of hand once it's all gotten big enough. At some point you may even want to consider outsourcing the work to firms that can handle parts of it for you. Hopefully you'll start doing that fairly soon through the use of such things as flyer distribution companies and telemarketers. Eventually, you may need more assistance, and it's a smart thing to invest in. Not only does outsourcing allow your systems to maximize their potential and run at full efficiency, but it also frees your time up to do nothing but sell. That's when the really big money starts to come in, and it's how the very top of the top producers operate to produce the dazzling results they do.

## ALWAYS FIND NEW WAYS TO PROSPECT

The self-marketing techniques presented in this book aren't the only methods out there. New and more effective ways to generate leads are coming about all the time. For example, blogs and video e-mail are two methods that are fairly new to me and that I've started using only recently. The results have been spectacular. I'm sure there are new, forward-thinking methods coming out that I don't know about yet. The point I'm trying to make is that you must always keep your eyes open and your mind receptive to new ideas. There may be a great new way to prospect that nobody has stumbled upon yet but that may be staring all of us in the face. Once you have all of these techniques working for you, start looking for new ones you can add!

## YOUR ONLY REAL ENEMY IS TIME!

Time is our single most precious asset, but it's the one asset that people tend to waste more than any other. The scary thing about wasting time is that once it's gone, it's gone forever and can never be replaced. At least if someone goes broke, the money can be made back. That's not the case with time.

The most frustrating thing for me in teaching and coaching sales-people has to do with the fact that so many of them will go through my programs and hear what I have to say, then go back to work without actually doing any of it. Others will go through my programs, then try one or two techniques for a couple of weeks, and finally go back to cold calling when they don't get immediate, spectacular results. I've literally had people ask for their money back because after completing one of my programs, they went out and threw some flyers around for two days but didn't get many leads from it. Don't be one of these people.

I urge you not to waste time when it comes to implementing this system of selling. Get started RIGHT NOW. If you don't do it now, while you're excited about the material and it's all fresh in your mind, the urgency will wear off and you'll never get around to doing it.

The following quote is by Napoleon Hill. It was first published in 1928, but the message is timeless. In fact, it's more applicable today than ever before in history. Time is becoming increasingly scarce and therefore more valuable as we continue to lead busier lives:

> TIME! Procrastination robs you of opportunity. It is a significant fact that no great leader was ever known to procrastinate. You are fortunate if AMBITION drives you into action, never permitting you to falter or turn back, once you have rendered a decision to go forward. Second by second, as the clock ticks off the distance, TIME is running a race with YOU. Delay means defeat, because no man may ever make up a second of lost TIME. TIME is a master worker which heals the wounds of failure and disappointment and rights all wrongs and turns all mistakes into capital, but, it favors only those who kill off procrastination and remain in ACTION when decisions are to be made. Life is a great checker-board. The player opposite you is TIME. If you hesitate you will be wiped off the board. If you keep moving you may win. The only real capital is

TIME, but it is capital only when used. Move by move TIME has wiped off Mr. Average Man's men until he is finally cornered, where TIME will get him, no matter which way he moves. INDE-CISION has driven him into the corner.

With that in mind, put this book down and get started RIGHT NOW! I would have achieved success a lot sooner had I only under-stood the real value of time and eliminated procrastination and indeci-sion from my life early on. Best of luck; I'll see you at the top!

# ABOUT THE AUTHOR

Frank J. Rumbauskas Jr. started his sales career cold calling to no avail, failing to make his numbers, only to receive the useless advice of "increase your activity" from managers. He then went into a trial-and-error period of several years and developed a complete system of selling that made him a top producer without cold calling. Author of the self-published sensation *Cold Calling Is A Waste Of Time*, Frank lives in Phoenix, Arizona, where he is a partner in several businesses including an insurance agency, a telecom services provider, and, of course, his sales training company, which strives to educate all salespeople that there are much better ways to prospect than cold calling. Frank's blog can be found at nevercoldcall.typepad.com.

# INDEX

Thank you for reading
*Never Cold Call Again:*
*Achieve Sales Greatness Without Cold Calling*

If you enjoyed this book, please take a look at
*The Sales Mastery Program*™,
a 4-CD audio program by Frank J. Rumbauskas Jr.

The Sales Mastery Program explains
advanced selling tactics that Frank himself used
to achieve an unheard of 80% close rate once he'd
perfected his lead-generation system.

It includes:
**Disc 1—Unstoppable Confidence**
**Disc 2—Ultimate Power and Control**
**Disc 3—Powerful Fact-Finding, Qualifying,**
**and Justification Techniques**
**Disc 4—Proposals and Presentations That Never Fail**

(All CDs are read by Frank himself.)

The program includes an accompanying guidebook
and reference manual, which you can download for free
at www.dontcoldcall.com in order to get an in-depth look
at what's covered in The Sales Mastery Program™.

For detailed information on The Sales Mastery Program, Frank's
coaching and consulting services, seminars, speaking, and
to subscribe to Frank's free newsletter, please visit:

**www.dontcoldcall.com**

Thank you!